Let Go!

"*The Secret of Letting Go* is a rare and welcome book—one that offers real solutions to real problems. And what wonderful solutions they are! They are not the standard, meaningless answers one usually hears. . . . this book makes it oh, so clear, that the only way to solve any difficulty is to no longer live in its level at all. The pained individual must transcend the self that we now know—the one that created the problem in the first place. And then, remarkably, Finley lays out a road map, filled with helpful and encouraging instructions for accomplishing the journey.

"This is exactly the kind of book that is needed today. . . . From international incidents, through environmental changes, right down to that disturbing fight we had with the person we live with—people feel that they and their lives are out of control. Fortunately, this book offers immediate help. There is only one thing we can, or need, to control—our own reactions. And the way to control our reactions is to LET GO.

"These are serious subjects, and yet the book is light, practical, and fun to read. From the breath-taking opening story to the memorable aphorisms at the end, this is a fast-paced book you'll want to go back to again and again.

"What could be more important to anyone's life than the search for the true self? Only by finding who we really are can any permanent meaning to life be found. What could be more necessary than a guide book to help in this search? This is eactly what Guy Finley has provided—a guide to self-discovery." **—Dr. Ellen B. Dickstein**

"The healing facts presented in this book have rescued me from more self-defeating pursuits and habits than I care to mention.

"This book is filled with the right tools for transforming troubles into triumphs. Guy Finley takes the Wisdom of the Ages and uses it to gently coach his readers to heal the places in their own minds where psychological problems originate. This book will help you if you are willing to follow the instructions.

"You will discover that you need not be dependent on anyone or anything for happiness; that all psychological stress—anger, depression, anxiety—is born out of a lack of understanding. Guy Finley's book is a very powerful and yet cheerful and lighthearted lesson in learning to let go of who you think you are." **—Desi Arnaz, Jr.**

About the Author

Guy Finley is the author of over eight books and books-on-tape, several of which have become international bestsellers. His writings are found in public libraries throughout the United States and his work is widely endorsed by doctors, celebrities, and leading professionals. He has enjoyed numerous successful careers, including composing award-winning music for many popular recording artists, motion pictures, and television programs.

In 1979, after travels to India and parts of the Far East in search of truth and higher wisdom, Guy voluntarily retired from his flourishing career in order to simplify his life and continue with his inner studies. He now lives in southern Oregon, where he gives ongoing talks on self-development.

To Write to the Author

Guy Finley lives and teaches in southern Oregon, where he speaks twice weekly about Higher self-development. If you would like to write him about this book or wish more information about his other works, please send a self-addressed stamped envelope to:

Guy Finley
P.O. Box 10P
Merlin, OR 97532

Visit Guy Finley's Life of Learning Foundation web site at:

www.guyfinley.com

Take part in his discovery-filled monthly chat room discussions, enjoy excerpts from his books, and get the latest news on continuing developments and special in-person appearances.

THE SECRET OF
LETTING GO

by

GUY FINLEY

Foreword by Desi Arnaz, Jr.

Introduction by Jesse R. Freeland, M.D.

Special Message from Vernon Howard

2000
Llewellyn Publications
St. Paul, Minnesota 55164-0383, U.S.A.

FIRST EDITION
Fourteenth printing, 2000

Cover Design by Christopher Wells and Terry Buske

Library of Congress Cataloging-in-Publication Data
Finley, Guy, 1949–
The secret of letting go / by Guy Finley; foreword by Desi Arnaz, Jr.; introduction by Jesse R. Freeland; special message from Vernon Howard.
p. cm.
ISBN 0-87542-223-3
1. Self-actualization (Psychology). 2. Success—Psychological aspects. 3. Happiness. I. Title.
BF637.S4F56 1990
158'.1—dc20 90-45794
CIP

Llewellyn Publications
A Division of Llewellyn Worldwide, Ltd.
P.O. 64383, St. Paul, MN 55164-0383
www.llewellyn.com

Printed in the United States of America

Contents

In Appreciation

To VH.

Other Books by Guy Finley

Success Without Stress
The Secret Way of Wonder
Freedom From the Ties That Bind
The Intimate Enemy
The Lost Secrets of Prayer
Design Your Destiny

Foreword

by
DESI ARNAZ, JR.

As someone who was — almost literally — born on a prime-time TV show *(I Love Lucy)*, I know first–hand that what the world calls success just isn't.

But don't get me wrong. I have no complaints about show business, Hollywood, my family, the public, or anyone else. In fact, I have no axe to grind about anyone or anything. The healing facts presented in this book have saved me from that particular kind of stress — including the useless business of blaming myself. And they have rescued me from more self–defeating pursuits and habits than I care to mention.

Life used to be, for me, a footrace against imaginary rivals. And the race — I found out — had no finish line; no tape that could be broken, and no prize. It was my boyhood friend — Guy Finley — who first introduced me to these wonderfully true and practical principles that have worked wonders in my life. My gratitude to him is beyond words.

Most self-development books have snappy titles and seemingly helpful approaches, but the reader's life remains as painful and bewildering as before. Such books are plentiful at rummage sales. *The Secret of Letting Go* will be hard to find at a rummage sale or second-hand bookstore. Good ideas that apply to one's everyday life are things we treasure and keep, like a comfortable pair of shoes or a favorite tool. This book is filled with the right tools for transforming troubles into triumphs.

In these pages, Guy Finley takes the Wisdom of the Ages and uses it to gently coach his readers to heal the places in their own minds where psychological problems originate. You have always sensed that help with emotional problems must be self-help anyway. Whether you are a whiz-kid, college graduate, or can barely read a sentence matters not at all. This book will help you if you are just willing to follow the instructions. In fact, I guarantee that if you work with these proven principles you will know more about your own mind — and therefore everyone else's — than the average Park Avenue psychiatrist. Believe me, I should know! Think of the savings in money alone! Among many other things, you will enjoy learning that life is a learning experience, as a school for our higher education, is a beautiful, inspiring, and immensely practical attitude. It equips a human being with an entirely different set of qualities that transforms stress to serenity, anxiety to assurance, and doubt to decisiveness.

From this bright book you will discover that you need not be dependent on anyone or anything for happiness; that all psychological stress — anger, depression, anxiety — is born out of a lack of understanding. Most significant for me was realizing that mental and emotional stress includes the deadly symptoms that manifest themselves as addictions. But you know, addictions can be very subtle. You tell me the difference between a person who is destroying their life with alcohol and someone who is destroying their life with fear, depression, or with being a "workaholic." The end result is the same — a life that doesn't work and one that ultimately destroys itself and everything around it. So I'm glad to say that, above all, Guy Finley's book is a very powerful and yet cheerful and lighthearted lesson in learning to let go of who you think you are. The principles being presented so pleasantly are deeper than the ocean.

Believe me, your heart already knows how right they are.

So be patient with your mind. It is an overworked, exhausted and confused veteran of useless battles against unnecessary enemies. Again, I should know!

I am a sober man now. For over nine years I have lived one day at a time. The important thing for me now is to continue walking away from myself, from my dependent nature. And I know I will succeed. Defeat has no right to exist. You will know this, too. Guy Finley's book, *The Secret of Letting Go,* is not an empty promise — it holds the keys to self-transformation — to an effortless New Life. Here is the solution to the mystery of why we were put on earth. Enjoy your life; enjoy the journey. I know you will.

Introduction

by
JESSE R. FREELAND, M.D.

People go to great lengths trying to believe and prove that emotional problems are caused by things outside of themselves. Other people, diet, lack of certain vitamins or minerals, past existences, heredity, viruses, family environment, air pollution — all are blamed. Billions are spent trying to find some answer to collective and individual distress. Nothing seems to work very well, does it? And that's because we have not diagnosed the cause.

The cause is simply individual; that is, personal lack of understanding of basic principles that have been all along waiting to protect, nurture, and gladden each of our lives. This tragic deficiency has rendered us exposed, vulnerable, and often lonely. In this book, we explore these life-solving principles from a much higher and more meaningful vantage point than usual. From that high hill, we can sight amazing and instructive disclosures about human nature.

One rather startling but healing fact I have learned — thankfully not too late — is that what I used to assume was "normal" is simply not. The assumption that the norm — or average man or woman — is at a healthy level of emotional development is the underlying mistake of at least this century in the fields of psychology, psychiatry, and sociology. I do not say this for shock effect or theatrics, but just to point out an elemental error that has caused horrendous distortions in our understanding of human nature. It is a basic blooper that makes most so–called research completely worthless. Surely if the average were normal, this planet would be a much happier place and most of its population would be untroubled, inwardly and outwardly happy and content individuals. The facts speak for themselves.

We must want to elevate our individual standards of inner health far above the so-called "normal." But first we must see that we have been, you and I, settling for unrecognized agony where there is really no need to settle for it. We can and must be more careful physicians for ourselves and allow this new self-study to lead us to its natural healing conclusion: The letting go of that lower, false nature within us that is so satisfied living in limitation and self-defeat. But knowing what we need to do and actually doing it are quite often two very different matters. "Letting go" is an ancient idea; a wise prescription. Letting go places the practicing individual within the flow of life instead of swimming against it.

However, most of what we call letting go today is really just picking up another thought or feeling; the embracing of a new sensation that temporarily distracts us from the internal or external conflict. Obviously, this is no real solution. To really see through and let go of our inner difficulties requires the formation of an interesting new kind of inward relationship with oneself. We can think of this for now as an ideal doctor-patient relationship.

The figure of the Doctor is crucial in this liaison because the Patient — the suffering false self — is a very ill creature capable of no real insight or curative influence on itself. Our personal inner Patient was treated badly in its formative years and so has become a supersensitive hypochondriac. No offense, but the original caretakers were quacks and confidence tricksters, themselves very ill and agonized beings. So, our Patient wrongly associates helpful correction with injury, loss of autonomy, and crushing of the spirit.

Thus, the job of Doctor in our quest for true success is a difficult one, rife with traps and pitfalls. Above all, the attitude and feeling of Doctor needs conscientious attention and awareness, for Patient is exquisitely sensitive to any sign of negative attitude or neurotic confirmation of its real existence and justification for its continued illness and mistrust.

So Doctor must have an attitude of objectivity — nonjudgmental, profoundly understanding, and clean of any personal stake in the progress of the case. Yet all the while, Doctor must be a supremely vigilant, diligent worker who is aware of everything going on in the "treatment."

In actual medical situations, especially in psychiatry and other forms of psychotherapy, it is easy for a therapist to become unconsciously impatient and "fed-up" with a difficult, hard-headed Patient. Of course, whenever that happens, all hope of cure is lost. If he loses control, Doctor has proved to be just like the old care-givers — and just like Patient, too. To Patient, it has been proven, in other words, that life is always the same; so what's the use? This would be a perverse victory for Patient, who has great mechanical skill in bringing out such reactions in order to confirm the "reality" of its conditioned false life.

So we see from all this that, for benefit to occur, Doctor must in a sense not just be Doctor but must treat even his very own self as another Patient who needs constant watching and understanding.

I know this seems complex, but our extra effort to understand it will pay off by providing a real diagnosis of the problem. Once the facts are in hand, then letting go becomes an incredibly natural and effortless healing act. We gladly watch as introduced negative emotions and reactions we were not born with start to fall away. So our inner situation really is like a large hospital of severely infected people, each inmate needing objective examinations and "patient" attention.

Doctor needs to have a keen sense of what is right and what is wrong, just as real, physical doctor's senses must be keenly tuned to detecting pathology—sickness of any kind. The doctor who faints at sickness, or who wants to pretend that everything is fine, that the patient is only slightly ill and will recover without outside help, is a bad doctor. Also, as indicated previously, a bad doctor is also one who refuses to see his own weakness and prejudices and, above all, who spurns the idea of getting a "consultation" (Higher Help).

No pun intended, but I love the phrase "Higher Patience" because it describes for me something otherwise quite inaccessible to ordinary language. It signifies something we must constantly invite within us with the right kind of quietness and, at the same time, alertness. The two simple words convey the wonderful and beneficial essence of True Spiritual Healing.

Dr. Jesse Freeland is a native of Lanarkshire, Scotland, and earned his medical degree at the University of Glasgow. He is a well-known writer and lecturer and his works have been published in USA Today, Westways, The Humanist, *and many other journals. A member of the AMA, APA, and several psychiatric organizations, Dr. Freeland has served as a consultant to the California State Rehabilitation Service and the University of California. Presently retired from private practice, he is the former Director of Psychiatry at the Devereux Foundation and Research Association at the University of California.*

How This Book Can Help You Let Go

I remember I once watched a young boy about to take his first lesson in water-skiing. He was bobbing up and down in the water, ski tops pointed up and ahead. His father was in the speedboat calling out some last-minute instructions. Then, with a roar, the boat took off. The tow rope went taut.

At first it didn't look like the young boy would make it up. But slowly, like some kind of glistening phoenix, he emerged from the water. He was up. I could see him smiling. Then, in almost the reverse motion of how the boy had risen above the water, he disappeared back into it. It didn't look like a bad spill.

The speedboat raced back around to pick him up. I waited and watched to see his small head pop up above the waves set off by his first nosedive — but none appeared. I saw why at the moment his father did. The boy was still holding on to the tow rope! He was being dragged behind the very boat that was trying to speed to his rescue. Assessing the situation in a glance, his father immediately cut the engines. A second later the young boy's soaked but smiling face raised itself out of the water and looked up to his father for the next instructions. His father smiled back and said, "Son, I forgot to tell you one very important point about water-skiing. When you fall, you must remember to let go of the rope!" They both laughed out loud at this lighthearted lesson because the need to let go was so obvious. I secretly laughed along with them.

I remember this incident so well because of the long-lasting impression it formed in me. I know that the reason why this young boy didn't let go of the tow rope wasn't that he wanted to hold on to it. No, he held on because he didn't know what else to do during those frightening moments he was being dragged through the water. For him, the thought of letting go wasn't an option at that moment. Instead, his mind was completely crowded with other competing thoughts and feelings, such as: "I hope no one else saw me make a fool of myself! What could have gone wrong? Is Dad gonna be mad at me? Will he let me try again? How could I be so stupid?" The instinctive and naturally intelligent thought that was telling him to let go couldn't get through all of this inner clamor. It was being blocked by a flood of misplaced and dangerous false self-concern. The reason I can report this event and its details with such certainty is that I was the young boy in the story, the boy who didn't let go. It was the first of many lessons in my own life about secret and self-defeating inner-forces that make a person hold onto something that he'd be better off letting go.

That's what this book is all about — letting go; letting go of everything that drags us through unpleasant relationships and events; letting go of those painful thoughts and feelings that sink our spirits with weary, false self-concerns.

At first, you may find this book strange and unsettling, for it is filled with surprising and higher insights that show you where you have been clinging to solutions that don't work. All of us suffer from holding on to one sorry situation or another — people pleasing, angry attitudes, wasteful wishes, harmful habits — just to name a few. But just because you haven't been able to let go of these persistent problems doesn't mean you can't. All it means is that you haven't as yet learned the secret of letting go. Here's a hint. One of the most exciting discoveries you will make as you read this book is that you don't need strength to let go of something. What you really need is understanding; and that's how this book will help you accomplish your lifelong dreams of being truly strong and independent. Step by step in helpful dialogues, probing questions and answers, and in Truth Tales packed with higher facts, you will learn about a special part of yourself that cannot be dominated or defeated by anything. This True Self always remains open and responsive and never holds onto any position other than the wish to learn what is true. This is its power. And this will be your power — an inexhaustible source of intelligence.

This new relationship with yourself will keep you safe and inspired forever. With each new insight you gain about yourself, your life-level is automatically lifted. To your endless delight, you discover that each higher view is more inspiring than the last and this encourages you to keep climbing in order to see more. This magical kind of relationship in life does exist and can be yours. You need only to want it more than you want to cling to the mountain where you presently are. Let go! You'll be so happy you did. I know it.

Above all, this is a bright book. With your permission and persistence, it can light in you the inner lamp that leads to true self-liberation. Of this I have no doubts. Totally free living is not an ideal. It must be our destination. And that brings us to my last note.

Nothing can or should ever be measured solely by its parts. If you were to take a masterpiece painting and concentrate upon only one of its brushstrokes or colors, you would miss not only the painter's intention but its beauty as well. What I am saying is that the sum of the whole canvas is greater than its parts. Its power and beauty remain an undefinable quality that is present only when the whole painting is viewed. The same holds true for the ideas in this book. We are trying to express something that thoughts and feelings simply can't convey because, as true or well-intended as they may be, they are, nevertheless, only the partial; one frame at a time of a living film that must be seen in its entirety if its meaning is to be understood and grasped. So it is of great importance that you don't so much read this book as allow it to sink in. You will see that, just as gentle rains bring the bounty and beauty of spring flowers, so will the Truths in this book bring you the secret of letting go.

Guy Finley
Ojai, California

CHAPTER 1

Let Go and Grow Happy

There was once an archaeologist whose entire life's work had been the tireless search for an ancient and mysterious temple. Stories passed down through generations of unsuccessful seekers told of almost unfathomable riches locked within its buried chambers. Yet no one had ever succeeded in uncovering the great temple and its secret treasures. That's why, as he stood there looking into the small, dark, earth-crusted opening in the vine-covered jungle hillside, the archaeologist knew that he mustn't let his imagination run wild.

But this had to be it. Everything in him knew it. Countless years of research pointed the way to this very spot.

Soon the archaeologist had enlarged the overgrown opening enough to crawl through. As he came to his feet, his pounding heart suddenly came to a dead stop. In the dim, dust-filled light of his kerosene lantern he could see, stretching out before him, a large, crude tunnel supported by hand-hewn timbers. It was obvious others had been there before him. Questions tumbled through his mind: Who had beaten him there? Why hadn't he already heard of its discovery? Had they plundered the temple's riches? Could he be mistaken about this location? But it was his keen eye that quieted his troubled thoughts. The tunnel ahead of him came to an abrupt dead end. Perhaps the secrets of the temple were still intact! Cautious further investigation showed that several chambers to the left and the right of the tunnel had only been partially excavated. What was going on? Why had they stopped short?

He had his answer a moment later as he gently leaned against one of the supporting timbers. He heard a loud creak, and soon small rocks and choking dust filled the air. He leaped for the opening, hoping to reach it before he was closed within forever, but his dive for the light came up short. To his surprise, it didn't matter. There was no cave-in; just the threat of one. He laughed out loud. Here was the reason the temple had lived on with its treasures unmolested. Over the centuries its vaults had filled in with seeping tropical earth, decaying vegetation and crumbled rocks too unstable to safely remove. The riches must still be there, if only he could find a way to reach them.

So, in spite of the obvious dangers, he decided to go ahead and continue excavating the long-abandoned site.

Over the months and years that followed, the archaeologist worked on — alone and in secret. It was slow going at best. The little progress he did manage each day had to be shorn up by an ever-increasing number of heavy support timbers. And, much to his growing dismay, a steadily increasing number of his work hours were spent just holding some of the older timbers in place. The sound of their almost uncontrollable creaking and sagging never left him alone. Even at night, outside the dig area and safely by his campfire, he could hear the timbers moan.

More than anything else, the archaeologist was tired. By this time he felt as if he had carried the whole inside of the mountain out on his back. And in a way he had. One by one he had nearly emptied the temple's inner chambers of the roots, rocks and earth that had filled them; and one by one that was all he found within them — roots, rocks and earth. He began to despair.

It was late the next afternoon, just before the close of another hard day of digging, when it started. The archaeologist wasn't concerned at first. He had already seen this kind of thing at least a hundred times before. One section of the post and beam timbers in the center of the excavation site suddenly started shifting. He ran over to its central set of supports and threw all of his weight against it to help hold it in place. As he stood there, braced between the earthen wall and clinging to the support timber, he realized that something beyond his control was starting to happen. He knew because he could hear it. The creaking beams directly over his head were not growing any quieter. In fact, like the sympathetic strings of some huge, ancient harp, each set of the massive overhead timbers all the way down the tunnel were now beginning to quiver and sing out one by one. It sounded as if the accumulated pressure of a thousand years was about to break loose.

The archaeologist started running from one set of shuddering posts to another, trying to dampen their accelerating pitch by using himself as a human brace. No good! Dirt and dust drifted in the air, making it hard to breathe and even harder to see. In mounting desperation and running out of options, he ran back blindly in the direction of the main tunnel. To have any chance of preventing a complete cave-in, he would need to stop this run–away reaction from overcoming the central set of supports. Calling upon what he knew was the last of his strength, he threw all of his weight up against one of the rough-hewn center posts just as it was about to collapse. For the moment it held. Then, the irony of what he realized might be his last mortal act brought a brief half-smile to his face. It was funny because *he* was supposed to be bracing the post; but in his heart he knew if that post weren't there to hold him up, he would surely be the one to fall over.

As amused as he was by this thought, he was even more

surprised by another thought that followed on its heels. It made absolutely no sense. He pushed it away as unthinkable. But just as his efforts to keep the tunnel's heavy posts in place were proving to be in vain, so was he unable to resist this one strangely persistent thought. "Why not just let go?" it kept asking.

He wondered if this was what it felt like to be losing his mind. Yet, as ridiculous as the idea of letting go seemed to be at that moment, there was something unbelievably compelling about it, so compelling that it almost demanded his complete attention. He felt like a man whose feet had accidentally stepped down one at a time into two different worlds — two worlds that were moving further and faster apart with each passing second. It was very clear that something was about to give. He fought to hold on to everything he'd always thought most important, yet it just didn't seem to matter anymore.

He wished he could understand what was happening in him, but it was as though the whole concern had been taken out of his hands. All he could do now was watch his own mind as it ran this way and that way, busily considering his options. On one hand, if he were somehow able to hold all this together and restabilize the support system, the only real certainty to be won for his efforts would be the promise of another dusty day — most of which would be spent working to hold everything together. He was so tired of finding one empty treasure room after another. On the other hand — and his back stiffened at this thought — if he did let go it would mean the end of his life-long work, the end of his hopes and dreams — maybe even the end of his life!

The sharp crack of an overhead timber near the mouth of the excavation entrance suddenly resolved the archaeologist's inner dispute. It was finished. He knew there was no point in trying to make it out and no point in trying to hold on. There was really nothing left to think about. He was glad. His next act came naturally. He just let go. Everything around him seemed to be in perfect order as the posts, timbers and supports all began spilling in on one another. The air became the earth. Standing there, right in the middle of what he thought was the end of his life, he felt fine — better than he could ever remember. "How strange," he thought — and then everything went dark.

As he lay there, his ears were the first part of him to awaken. At least that is how it seemed. It felt as if they were almost straining to hear something — but what it was they were listening for the archaeologist had no idea. Everything was so wonderfully quiet, and he didn't want to open his eyes for fear of disturbing the strange silence.

Another awareness came calling for his attention. Now he remembered where he was — and what had happened. Somehow he had been spared. A quick sensory check of his body told him that everything was in place and all right. It was time to move. He carefully pushed his upper body up and out of the earth until he was sitting upright. With his eyes still closed, he shook the dirt out of his hair and prepared himself to look upon the collapsed and crumbled ruins of his life's work. He opened his eyes.

Support timbers lay every which way, as if someone had dropped a handful of giant wooden matches on the ground. The archaeologist slowly lifted his gaze higher in order to take in more of his surroundings. Nothing could have prepared him for what his weary eyes were about to see. It was too fantastic.

He shook his head again to see if he was dreaming, but the dull throbbing in one of his partially buried legs told him he was very much awake. It was no wonder the riches of the temple had never been found. No wonder this great and ancient mystery had gone unsolved for all of these ages. The flood of his racing thoughts were interrupted by a burst of his own uncontrollable laughter. It echoed back at him as if to confirm some great joke. Everyone who had ever been there before him, looters and scientists alike, all had been searching in the wrong places and looking for the wrong things. The archaeologist laughed aloud again and arched his neck all the way back to look straight up.

High above his head, suspended like a star-studded golden sky, was the great vaulted dome of the temple: A vast dome made of solid gold inset with jewels of all colors and sizes. The cave-in he thought was going to take everything from him had instead revealed the Secret of Secrets: The temple's treasure had never been stored *in* the temple. *The real treasure was the temple itself!* And now it belonged to him to enjoy as his pleasure and to take at his leisure. He silently thanked the heavens for giving him the courage to let go.

You too possess a priceless secret that awaits your discovery. This is what *The Secret of Letting Go* is all about.

This Isn't Letting Go

Merely wanting to let go of an unhappy circumstance or nagging emotional ache is not enough. Wants are desires, and desires replace one another like bees waiting in line at an open flower. That is why it is so important for us to deeply understand what letting go is all about.

Let's start with what we do know, or at least, with what we should know about letting go. By now we should know what letting go *isn't.* This time-honored approach — discovering what something isn't in order to come upon what it is — is a powerful method for coming upon the Truth. Great mystics, wise men and scientists of all ages have long understood the value of arriving at what is true by first revealing and then eliminating what is false. Let's follow their wise counsel and look at letting go in this new way.

1

Letting go isn't living with the heartache-filled dreams of what might have been.

2
Letting go isn't the certainty that somebody else was wrong.

3
Letting go isn't moving on from one disappointment to the hope of some new victory.

4
Letting go isn't the anxious search for a new solution to an old problem.

5
Letting go isn't learning to live with lowered expectations.

6
Letting go isn't the avoidance of people or places that painfully remind you of past attachments.

7
Letting go isn't having to convince yourself of how right you were to let go of something.

8
Letting go isn't the desperate search to find someone to agree with you about your side of an argument.

9
Letting go isn't the need to rehearse conversations in your mind in an attempt to feel confident.

10
*Letting go isn't your insistence that you can let go of (*fill in the blank*) anytime you want.*

There is one more point to ponder while on our revealing investigation of what letting go isn't. Letting go has nothing in common with self-sacrifice and the sour or resentful feelings that always seem to accompany any of our self-designed acts of self-denial. So, in brief review, we can see that letting go has nothing to do with disciplines, the external rearrangement of our affairs, or struggling to be free in our relationships. In fact, letting go has nothing to do with the release of anything outside of yourself. It never has.

We all know exactly what it is like to be certain we have let go of something sorrowful or worrisome, only to find ourselves in a similar sad situation moments later. Dropping this person and picking up that person doesn't end the loneliness that drives us into dead-end relationships. This isn't letting go. We have only managed to put the emptiness on hold. Changing jobs to get away from someone or something that sets us off doesn't cancel our conflict. This just delays the inevitable angry feelings that always surface whenever we feel threatened. Our anger cannot keep us safe from an insensitive world — this anger is the insensitivity itself.

The Greatest Secret on Earth

The truth is that letting go is very simple and, above all, natural; as natural for you and I as it is for a tree to shed the heavy, sun-ripened fruit that clings to its branches. Why? Because both man and tree, in fact all living things, are created to drop what is no longer needed. For the tree, the falling fruit carries its matured seed to the ground. No unnatural force is necessary. In a similar fashion — that is to say, under higher but equally exacting laws — these same friendly forces are waiting to do for you what you haven't been able to do for yourself. You need only learn to cooperate with these powerful and timeless principles to be able to let go of any emotional bitterness, relentless regret, anxious worry or troubling thought. The rest will be done for you.

This is what the secret of letting go is all about. First must come the understanding that we are still carrying around the accumulated defeats of a lifetime and that these weary weights have only served to make us someone sorry, not someone special. This initial shock may shake us, but it is really a major breakthrough. It heralds the first in a series of miraculous self-separations, in which we begin to see that we have been living from an unseen part of ourselves: A self that thinks clinging to wreckage is the same as being rescued! Now we understand why all of our past efforts to let go have only left us holding a new problem. But now we also know, at last, exactly what it is that must be dropped. We must let go of this sorry self that is certain it is better to suffer and *feel* like someone than it is to just let go and quietly *be* no one. Have no concerns how this task will be accomplished. That is Reality's responsibility.

This higher knowledge that is now beginning to reveal you to yourself is *not* mental. It is coming to you from a lofty, wise and powerful part of yourself which lives way above everyday thinking and its ceaseless conflict over what may or may not be best. Your newly awakening inner-nature *knows* what is best for you because it *sees* life without the painful confusion and contradictions that always accompany compulsive self-interest. For instance, this higher intelligence knows that you don't need to ache even when you are sure you must. Once you have made contact with this still secret self within, it does the rest. That's right. It is this higher part of yourself alone that has the strength and wisdom to gently open your hand so that out of it may drop all that has been making you unhappy.

Believe me, you are on the verge of the single greatest discovery any human being can make. The secret of letting go not only holds the keys for ending what is unwanted, but locked within this same supreme secret is the beginning of your New Life —the birth of a new nature that never has to hold on to anything because it is *already everything*. Dare to proceed. Let the following special insights speed you on your way.

1
Letting go of yourself is letting go of your problems, for they are one and the same.

2
Go along with your longing to be limitless.

3
Uncovering what is wrong must always precede the discovery of what is right.

4
You can only be as free as you are willing to be truthful about yourself.

5
Letting go is strictly an inside job.

6
There is nothing hidden in the world from the man who will reveal himself to himself.

7
You can live from *true intelligence or with self-insistence.*

8
Letting go takes no strength — only a willingness to see the need for it.

9
We can never act any higher toward a situation than our understanding of that situation.

10
Once you see *the problem, you know the solution.*

11
A weakness detected is a weakness rejected.

12

Letting go is the natural release which always follows the realization that holding on hurts.

13

Unhappiness does not come at *you, it comes* from *you.*

14

Suffering is only something you picked up by mistake.

15

What you really want is to stop thinking about yourself.

16

Defeat comes from clinging to solutions that don't work.

17

Letting go happens effortlessly when there is no other choice.

18

Real freedom is the absence of the self that feels trapped, not the trappings that self acquires to make it feel free.

19

Wanting to learn about yourself while limiting your discoveries to what you want to find is like saying "I want to see the whole world from my bed."

20

The only thing you lose when you let go of something you are afraid to live without is the fear itself.

Be Stronger Than Anything That Frightens You

"I want to be brave when it comes to cutting myself loose from self-destructive situations, but each time I even get close to letting go I get really scared. And when I get scared I seem to hold on to everything even tighter! Is there a way to get past this fear? I loathe the idea that I may be too frightened to find freedom."

"Yes. There is a way past this part of yourself that would rather hold on than get out. However, to really let go of these fears we must first go *through* them."

"But I have tried overcoming my fears, and fight as I might, I just can't seem to break free of their dark and self-limiting influences."

"That's because you're trying to dominate the fear."

"Well, what else do you do with something that won't let go of you? Don't you have to find a way to be stronger than it?"

"Yes, of course, but fighting with fear is like trying to deliver a knock-out punch to a scary shadow. All you do is wear yourself out. To flatten your fears once and for all, you must forget about the idea of domination and start thinking about illumination."

"Illumination? What do you mean?"

"I mean self-illumination: The miracle that happens within us whenever we dare place the wish to *understand* what is frightening us before our certainty that there is no other choice but to feel afraid."

"I like the sound of what you're saying, but tell me, how can what I understand cancel the fear I feel?"

"Because if you will dare to go ahead and be just as

frightened as you really are, but at the same time agree to meet these fears consciously, you will actually see that what is so shaky is *not* you!"

"Please — I would like to know more about this new understanding."

The seemingly scary condition, whatever it may be, is not the problem. It is your *reaction* that is fearful. This is why if you will become *conscious* of your condition instead of afraid of it, you will change forever your relationship with fear. It is only within this special kind of inner-relationship that there is real safety, because now you are interacting with fear in an entirely new way. You are no longer letting it dictate to you how to act or what to do. Instead, you are aware of the fear. You are studying it, and as each day you discover something new about the strange and shaky nature of your own fearful reactions, they begin to lose their power over you.

Why? Because you are at last seeing them for what they have always been: Unintelligent mechanical forces. You are slowly becoming stronger than they are because by seeing them as they are — not as they would have you see them — you have helped yourself to climb above and outside of their influence. This self-insight is the difference between trembling through your life and being in command of it.

To be consciously afraid means that *you know you are frightened*, but at the same time you know that these very fears, as real as they may seem, are not *you*. And no wrong reaction can keep you captive once you begin to see it for what it is. Fear is, and has always been, nothing but a self-limiting reaction that we cling to in the darkness of our present life-level, having mistaken it for a shield of self-protection. But, just as the faintest of early morning sunlight can dispel the night-long darkness, so does the smallest of insights into a persistent fear lead to letting it go.

You can prove this powerful principle to yourself anytime you want. Just dare to proceed even while being afraid. But remember, your new aim isn't to be courageous or to try and act strong in the face of fear. No. We've seen that this won't work. You simply want to be more curious about your frightened thoughts and feelings than you want to believe in them. If you will follow this simple but Higher Instruction, not only will you start to *see* these habitual reactions that have been keeping you scared and running, you'll actually start seeing *through* them. This is where the real miracle occurs. Each new insight into the actual nature of these negative reactions removes some of their power over you. And their loss is your gain. You are stronger now and you know it. You also know this new strength will never fail you because it isn't just the temporary appearance of a bold opposite. This new strength of yours is the *absence* of an old weakness.

Let's look at just one of the ways in which this principle of putting self-illumination before psychological self-protection can turn fear into fearlessness. Do you know someone that you would rather run from than run into? Most of us do! Nevertheless, starting right now, resolve never again to avoid any person that scares you. In fact, go ahead and walk right up to that critical man or aggressive woman and say or do exactly what *you* want instead of letting the fear tell you to do what *it* wants. Have no ideas at all about the way things should or shouldn't go. You are there to watch and learn about yourself, not to win an ego victory. Let that person see you shake if that is what starts to happen. What do you care? Besides, it is only temporary. That unpleasant person before you can't know it, but you are shaking yourself awake.

For the first time, you are letting your reactions roll by instead of letting them carry you away. As you stand there, momentarily apart from your usual self and working hard to remain as inwardly watchful as you know how, you can see that this flood of previously unconscious reactions has its own life story; a shaky sort of story that up until now you had embraced as your own. But now you are beginning to see the whole story. The fears do not belong to you. Here is the explanation.

You have never been afraid of another person. The only thing you have ever been frightened by is *your own thoughts* about that person. Yes, you did *feel* fear, but it wasn't yours and it wasn't towards someone stronger than you. The fear you felt was in what you *thought* he or she was thinking about you. Amazing isn't it? You have been afraid of your own thoughts! And seeing this ends this. Now you can let this thought-self go, because no one holds on to terror.

The Sure Way to Raise Your Life Level

As we will eventually come to see, almost every kind of unhappy feeling is the result of mistaking the partial for the whole. What this means is that when we don't see the whole picture, we are likely to act in a way that is self-defeating. One example of this would be that terrible sinking feeling that comes with learning too late, after you've become upset, that things weren't the way you were so sure they had been. That, in fact, it was you who had misjudged or misunderstood the person or event; and now that you can see the whole situation, there is no reason at all to be angry or sad, anxious or afraid. How many times have we regretted some thoughtless action on our part once we found out all of the facts? This is what we must do: gather all of the facts. I promise you that everything can be explained. Nothing that happens to you or through you need ever go without you understanding why. You can be self-enlightened instead of self-frightened. You have a choice. This discovery that you can always choose in favor of yourself is real excitement.

You do not have to accept your present life-level. Life-level is what determines whether you sail through this life or sink in it. At present, it may seem to you as if there are times when you don't have much choice in your own life. I want you to know that this is a lie. This temporary feeling of being trapped is part of your current life-level, where you sincerely feel as though your choices are limited. Again, I want you to know this is simply not true. There is always a choice.

The problem is that most men and women insist upon *their choices*. You must see this. Your present life-level has been determined by the choices you have *already* made. Why go back to the same field of choices? You already suspect that it will yield no real harvest of happiness. Go ahead and confirm your suspicion. Nothing bad will happen to you. In fact, only something good can occur once you stop clinging to useless ideas. You could say that your new choice is to stop choosing for yourself *from* yourself. This is the first necessary step for changing your life-level. Here is something to help you see the wisdom of your new and higher choice.

If your choices so far have left you feeling dissatisfied and incomplete, you must stop blaming your selections and see that *the problem lies with the chooser—you!* You and what happens to you every day are the reflections of your life-level. We are wrongly led to believe that life makes us into the kind of person we are. The truth is that the kind of person we are, our life–level, makes life what it is for us! This is why nothing can really change for us until we see that our unhappiness isn't connected with the event, it is the level of it. Let's look at this a little more deeply.

We believe that we meet events and that those events are good or bad, pleasurable or punishing. In other words, our feelings are the reflections of what happens to us moment to moment. That's why, while acting from our current life-level, our first choice whenever we feel distressed is always to try and change the condition we blame for making us feel that way. The belief being that by changing our unhappy surroundings we will bring an end to our unhappiness. This has never really worked, and it never really will, because *the unpleasant or unhappy condition was not the event but your reaction to it.*

What does this new knowledge mean to you? Everything! It means:

1

You can let go of those resentful feelings toward your job, because the treadmill isn't what you are doing but the way you are thinking.

2

You can let go of trying to change other people, because you *are what is bothering you about them.*

3

You can let go of the fear of unforeseen changes or challenges because the only thing you really ever have to face is yourself.

Best of all, you can let go of the impossible and unbelievably self-punishing task of thinking that you are responsible for the way the world turns. The only world you are responsible for is your inner–world; the world of your thoughts and feelings, impulses and desires. Your life-level is determined by how clearly you can see into this inner-world. This new kind of seeing is safety and ultimately the root of all self-success, because when you know where not to step, your walk through life is a safe and happy one.

You wouldn't go over to your neighbor's kitchen to fix *your* broken sink. Why try and change your outer world when it is only a reflection of your inner life? Do not try to change the external world. Change your own attitudes and viewpoints. When you change yourself, you change the world as far as you are concerned, for you are your own world. Here is a simple way to say all of this: *The inner determines the outer.*

This is not as difficult to understand as it may appear at

first. Let's take an example. If a person writing a letter misspells a word, the error starts in his mind, after which it appears on paper. He cannot possibly correct the paper until his mind is corrected first. If he does not clarify his mind, the error must repeat itself on paper endlessly. No doubt you see the parallel here with human problems. People try to correct exterior mistakes instead of correcting the way they think, which leaves them lost, because unknowingly they are still chained to a mistake-making machine. That is why it is so important to understand this lesson. Your discontentment with life is with your understanding — your life-level — not with what your understanding has brought to you. Trying to change your life without first changing your life-level is like trying to convince yourself that a merry-go-round has a destination. If you are tired of going around and around, remember that you can get off whenever you choose.

Truthful principles such as these are here to assist you in making this Higher choice by helping you to increase your self-understanding. This elevated understanding in turn raises your life-level. As you raise your life-level, you will see that you have effortlessly raised the way in which you react to every event. Then the whole world begins to slow down for you because you now understand that it wasn't this life that was making you dizzy — it was your thinking.

Go Ahead and Let Go Of Yourself

Any human being who has to hold himself together is someone who is ready to fall apart. Trying to hold yourself together is a terrible way to go through life. Our task is to prove this to ourselves. The fears of falling apart can never be quieted by adding more pieces to your self, such as success or the hopes of success. With this approach to life you wear out faster, because you now have even more conditions you believe you must control in order to keep your life together. Consider closely the following higher self-insight. It reveals the intelligence behind your wish to let go.

Anything that you have to control, controls you. The problem with self-control is that it is part of a war inside of you. No one ever wins in a war! Let's look at this same idea again from a slightly different perspective. Whenever an uncertain situation arises, the mind works feverishly to resolve it in order to regain a sense of being in control. However, the more feverishly the mind works, the more out of control you become! You can see this for yourself. Anything that is afraid of losing control is already out of control: An accident waiting to happen. There is more, and we must see it all if we are ever going to rise above our present life-level to true self-certainty.

Whenever we picture ourselves, there is one image that rarely if ever enters into our mental movie; that of being someone who is ready to fall apart. But again, few of us see ourselves in any self-compromising light at all. We feel safe within the dimly lit theatre of our own circle-of-self pictures and we return to it often — especially when the harsh light of reality starts to break through and show us that we may not be as together as we'd like to think. This is why we need the Truth in our lives. The Truth is what allows us to see reality without being frightened about what we see. Part of the Truth's rescuing action is to reveal to us that we are not apart from what we see. From this unique inner-vantage point, the light of reality isn't harsh — it's Home. The more of this light we can welcome into our circle-of-self and its cast of 1,001 self-images, the easier it becomes to let go. Why? Because we aren't losing anything except for what has been keeping us in the darkness.

If we are honest, we realize that our lives seem to grow smaller as we grow older. We have fewer friends, fewer activities; we take fewer and fewer risks. But why? Why should a person's possibilities for new and stimulating impressions diminish with their age? Why, if we are continuing to develop and grow as we should be, shouldn't we be looking for greater and greater personal challenges instead of avoiding them? Could this slowly constricting life of ours be the result of an unconscious urge on our part to avoid any situation or relationship that might toss the proverbial straw onto the camel's back of our picture of ourselves?

"I can see the logic of what you are saying, but as you said, I don't think this applies to me."

"Are you willing to see if it does?"

"Of course."

"Good. Do you ever get angry or anxious?"

"Yes I do, but what does that have to do with falling apart?"

"Let's see. What makes you angry or anxious?"

"When things don't go the way I want them to."

"In other words, you've pictured how things should be, and when life doesn't confirm these pictures, you get negative in one way or another."

"Yes, that about describes it. What are you getting at?"

"Let's work together at this. You said that when life doesn't confirm your self-pictures, your hopes of future security, love in relationships, whatever, then some kind of stress or unhappiness comes up as these pictures of yours begin to fall apart?"

"Please proceed."

"This shows us that within your present way of thinking you believe your future happiness actually depends upon these pictures. This is why, as your pictures begin to crumble, *so do you!*"

"Yes, but why do I get angry or anxious?"

"Because these punishing emotions are part of a subtle system of self-subterfuge that accomplishes two dark things at once. It keeps the problem alive and at the same time it keeps the real solution out of sight."

"What is the problem?"

"Essentially, it is a lack of understanding about your True Nature. You are about to discover that you are not who you think you are. No matter how attractive or repulsive, you are not any picture you may be holding of yourself."

"And what is the real solution?"

"Go ahead and let yourself fall apart!"

"What? That's going to take some explanation!"

"And there is one if you will *go through the experience*; but for now, here is the intelligence behind this unexpected answer. *You are not what will fall apart.* Who you truly are can never fall apart. What will collapse is the haunted house of self-flattering and security-seeking pictures you had mistakenly identified as a solution to your shaky life. These pictures are not the solution to your shakiness. *They are the source of it.*"

The Secret of Effortless Happiness

Have you ever noticed just how unhappy you can get over the fact you are not happy? Unexamined, this behavior seems to make sense. But a closer look at it will reveal that being unhappy over being unhappy is like throwing gasoline on a fire to put it out. You get lots of fire and smoke — even a strange excitement — but in the end all you are left with is ashes. This is why you must understand this next amazing fact.

You can make yourself miserable, but you can't make yourself happy.

This shouldn't be too much of a surprise. Even now we are learning that we have been unconscious conspirators in our own unhappy lives. Even if it wasn't being pointed out, most of us can admit that at times we do make ourselves miserable. But there is nothing good about feeling bad. There is never a justification for tolerating self-misery, because what is self-induced can be self-reduced and ultimately eliminated if you are willing to understand the underlying causes. This is why we must look at why it is impossible to *make* ourselves happy if we ever want to come upon *authentic* happiness.

Outside of drugs and alcohol, which are obviously not the way to happiness, whenever you want to *make* yourself happy, you must put forth an effort of some kind. Effort implies the application of force in a specific direction. We can see that this is good and necessary in following preconceived plans for construction projects, business concerns or cooking, for example. You can also make an effort to imagine or visualize new shapes and ideas to help in the creative process. But when it comes to being happy, *any effort* is the wrong one. Let's see if this is true. If it is, then we are on the verge of an even higher discovery: Real happiness is effortless. Let's find out more about this new possibility.

As we described, where there is an effort, there is, whether known or not, always a plan. All plans by definition are to build something; in this instance your plans are to build happiness. With this preconceived plan, this picture of happiness firmly fixed in your mind, you meet each of life's events looking for your picture instead of experiencing what life has brought to you. This painful and stress-producing process of comparison goes on unknowingly and it ruins everything it touches. Life becomes a series of disappointments instead of a series of happy adventures. Please ponder this next point. You could never be unhappy with anything you found in this life if you didn't already have it fixed in your mind what you were looking for.

Hopefully, we can learn from this that our ideas about happiness are more often than not the very root of our unhappiness. The point is that happiness cannot be made. It is not the result of anything. Happiness comes to those who understand that you can't seek it any more than you seek the air you breathe. It is a part of life to be found within living. The excitement of anticipation is not happiness, any more than smelling freshly baked bread nourishes a hungry body. All pursuit of happiness is based upon the false assumption that happiness can be possessed. It cannot. Happiness is the natural expression of a stress-free life, just as sunlight naturally warms the earth after dark clouds disappear.

Ten Steps to Take to the Truly New Life

The difference between being in true self-command and merely appearing that way is the difference between gently floating downstream and being swept away in waves of self-doubt. Higher Ideas such as these lead to the truly new life. Take them all the way to yourself.

1. *Study the situation by entering into it.*

2. *Be in charge, not in conflict.*

3. *Realize the need for self-correction.*

4. *Go conscious, not crazy.*

5. *Face fear's full bluff.*

6. *See that your reactions are not reality.*

7. *Be self-enlightened, not self-frightened.*

8. *Don't feel yourself, be yourself.*

9. *Self-rescue without self-revelation is self- deception.*

10. *Happiness is letting go of your ideas about happiness.*

CHAPTER 2

Your True Nature is High

There is nothing wrong with being a successful human being. In fact, the purpose of your life is to win. But what if, in your quest for this victory, you were accidentally drawn into a compelling game in which, unknown to you, it was impossible to win, no matter how well you performed or how religiously you followed the rules? Where, instead of finding the freedom to run as you wish, you found yourself moving more and more mechanically through your days — and each of these days left you feeling more frustrated than fulfilled, because you were playing under an ever-increasing pressure to succeed!

As if this sorry state weren't bad enough, whenever you looked around to see how the other players were doing, it was obvious they were just as disappointed with the game as you. No one was really winning anything!

Then one day, to your great shock and amazement, you discover that along with everyone else out there on the playing field, you had been tricked into taking part in a crazy game in which the rules you were taught to play by allowed you to score but never to stop running! You could compete but never achieve any meaningful or lasting victory.

This metaphor provides us with an uncompromising glimpse into our own present life-position. And precisely because it is an uncompromising view, it not only tells us why our days can feel so futile, but it also hints at a previously unthinkable solution to our sad situation. Maybe there is a way to win, after all!

For the first time we begin to understand why, in spite of our best efforts to come out on top, we are so often thrown for a loss in our relationships and everyday affairs. When these defeats pile up, life seems more of a punishment than a pleasure. We want to give up and walk away. But we can't. The rules we've been taught and play by don't cover or even acknowledge the possibility of life off of the field. We feel stuck. And so, little by little, just like the slow but steady drop in temperature that chills you without your knowing it, giving up just happens. We stop caring about the lasting things that make life good and noble, and start hoping for those little moments that make life on the field seem tolerable.

Listen. *Don't give up*. You don't have to. You can win in a brand new way. How? Just let go!

Let go of all the familiar but useless rules of rigor that tell you life would be meaningless without running around in some kind of conflict. Stop referring to your own well-worn but useless wish that your life will get better the longer you play. It won't — unless we believe that feeling exhausted is the same as being exalted. This is why we must start *seeing* the facts.

Yes, let go. Walk away. Nothing can stop you. Believe me, this is your first in a long series of real winning actions. Never mind what direction to take. It doesn't matter, not in the slightest. Why? Because walking away from what is false is the same as heading towards what is true. It may not seem so at the outset, but for the first time in your life the Rules of Life will be working *for* you. Here is how it works: Letting go of what holds you down is how you cooperate with going up. You see, your True Nature is high. And this is your new destination. But *you* don't choose it. No. You allow yourself to rise. This may feel awkward, even frightening at first, but in time you will recognize it as your natural need.

Learn to cooperate with the real Rules of Life, with Truthful Principles, and let them lift you. That is their job. Once we stop choosing to lose, winning in life takes place effortlessly. It is that simple. Henri Frederic Amiel, the mystic Swiss author and philosopher, understood the importance of placing ourselves in line with these Real Rules, and described what our lives are like when we don't.

> *"He who floats with the current, who does not guide himself according to higher principles, who has no ideal, no convictions—such a man is...a thing moved, instead of a living and moving being—an echo, not a voice. The man who has no inner–life is a slave of his surroundings as the barometer is the obedient servant of the air.*

Choose In Favor of Your True Self

"But you can't be saying I should walk away from everything I have worked for all my life?"

"No, I'm not. What I am saying is that we need to take a much closer look at what we have been calling our life."

"To what purpose?"

"To see if it is really ours. Once we know what is authentically our own, then we also know what to keep and protect and what to let go."

"I can understand this idea, but how does it apply to my life?"

"Let's look briefly at a true story from mother nature for some added insight. The cuckoo bird is best known for laying its eggs in the nests of other birds and leaving them there to hatch. She hides and waits until the nesting bird flies away, leaving its eggs unguarded. The cuckoo then swoops down and quickly lays one of her own so that when the unsuspecting parent returns to the nest it dutifully nestles down on what it believes to be its own clutch of eggs. Generally what happens next is the cuckoo chick hatches first and pushes the later, weaker hatchlings out of the nest. In this way, the parent birds, not realizing the switch has occurred, spend their energies nurturing and being responsible for something that doesn't belong to them."

"I like the story, but I'm not sure what you are trying to tell me."

"We too have been tricked into caring for a life that isn't really ours by unconsciously adopting a kind of substitute self. Always hungry for sensations and indiscriminate as to what kind, this self cares nothing for us outside of what we can bring to it. This shadowy inner-self has convinced us that what it wants is what we need. Over the years it has displaced, one by one, our natural inclinations to seek self-wholeness with its own unnatural drives for self-stimulation and self–preservation."

"So that's why you say I should go ahead and walk away from my life — it may not even be mine! To tell you the truth, there have been more than a few times when I can remember feeling as though my life didn't belong to me. Does that make sense?"

"Yes, we have all had those kind of unexplainable feelings

at one moment or another. But as there was no way at the time to understand the importance of their brief appearance, we learned to just ignore them until they faded. Well, the purpose of Truthful Principles such as the ones we'll be investigating in this book are to reawaken these all-but-forgotten Higher Feelings that doubt our present self. Welcome their faint stirring even if it means having to bear a temporary disturbance within you. These intuitive feelings are coming to you from a part of your True Nature that wants you to stop working against yourself and start learning in favor of who you really are."

Let the following Higher Hints help you to choose in favor of your True Self.

1

Whatever we are driven to win can never lead to true victory, because anyone who is driven to do anything is being whipped along by forces outside of himself. This is the definition of a slave, not a conqueror.

2

Revealing yourself to yourself is choosing in favor of your True Self.

3

If personal happiness is the measure of an individual's success, then anything that causes that person pain cannot be part of that success.

4

Suffering now so that you can be happy in the future makes as much sense as throwing yourself overboard so that later you can feel relief about being rescued.

5

Any want that is compulsive can never be a source of real

pleasure, since anything you are compelled to want makes you a servant of that very drive. There is very little pleasure in being pushed through life.

6

Learn to listen to any feelings that cast doubt on your need to suffer.

7

Asking to see more about a painful situation is the same as asking how you can let it go.

8

Walking away from the problems you don't want in your life gets easier each time it becomes clearer to you who you *don't need to be.*

9

You cannot be directed to decide against yourself without first being deceived into thinking that what hurts you can also help you.

10

True self-certainty is the absence of false self-doubt.

You Are Not Who Think You Are

During a class I was giving on "Letting Go of Self-Doubt," Pat S. wanted to know why unforeseen events, or even the threat of an unforeseen event, made her feel so uncomfortable. Following are the key questions and answers from our discussion:

Q: Why am I so easily upset by the unexpected?

A: If you're interested enough in this question, we can go into it. The answer may surprise you.

Q: Yes, I really want to know why changes in my life, at work or at home, make me so uneasy.

A: Good. Then let's start by clearing up the initial mental mistake that is at the root of your problem. *It's not really you* who feels shaky when situations shift without warning.

Q: If it's not me, then who is it?

A: Who you *think* you are. That's what feels threatened, but you don't have to go on feeling afraid. Beginning right now, with some patient self-investigation and the aid of a few higher facts, you will discover that you are not who you think you are. This is one of the most exciting and relief-filled self-findings you can make about yourself.

Living from our present life-level, we are almost always nervous about what's going on around us. Why? Because we still live with the mistaken notion that *who* we are is somehow affected or determined by *what happens* to us. This is like thinking that because you have a fender-bender, you are an automobile. Obviously, you are not your car. And yet, putting aside the light humor that our inner-confusion is apt to cause, there is nothing funny about thinking that you are going to lose yourself if someone leaves you. Just ask anyone who has ever gone through the nightmare of seeing a loved one walk away. *This* is why we are going to leave behind us, once and for all, this threatened nature of ours. By placing ourselves in the care of Real Intelligence, we can learn to let go of whatever it may be that has frightened us up to now. That's right. The winds of this world can blow hot or cold, gentle or like gales, and it won't matter to you. You have found yourself. Let's continue to learn.

There is only one possible explanation for how who you *really* are could ever get confused or pained by what happens to you. Simply stated, you are suffering from a case of *mistaken identity*. This identity crisis is born out of believing that who you are, your essential self, is somehow tied to the *events* in your life. This kind of thinking tends to make you afraid of almost any change in life. By thinking that your life is determined by events, you grow afraid of losing control of yourself if you can no longer control the events. Looking for yourself outside of yourself — whether through career, hobbies, or in the faces of people, family or strangers — is like trying to find your reflection in a tumbling mountain brook. You might see yourself for a flash, only to disappear. And then you must look again . . . and again . . . and again. Living from this unfortunate kind of mistaken identity leaves you endlessly on edge and hopelessly searching for yourself; a search that never ends because, just as the mountain brook dances ever onward, so is constant change the true nature of life.

Remember this next helpful idea and work to learn the intelligence behind it: *Events may happen to you, but you are not the event*. Just as clouds are not the sky, you are not what moves through you. You are not who you think you are.

As we have discovered, thinking that you are the event, being identified with it, gives rise to a certain wrong identity — an anxious and uncertain one. This mistaken identity is called the *false self* and it wears many hats. We are going to learn all about it and, at the same time, learn how to let go of it. If you will dare to let go of who you think you are, you will discover what life would be like if you had wings. This lower, false nature has lived unchallenged for a long, long time. Today, right now, is the beginning of the end of it and the true beginning of who you really are.

A Case of Mistaken Identity

Once a man awoke to find himself in a room he didn't quite recognize. Nothing was certain except for an unexplained dizzy feeling. All around him were mirrors, closets, and tables with trays of different colored makeup. The place was familiar, but what was he doing there? Anxiety began to seep in as he struggled to remember. But remember what? This was obviously the dressing room of some large playhouse, but what was his role? Each time he looked into the mirror he felt a stab of pain, because he wasn't quite sure who was looking back at him. He felt suddenly alone.

Not knowing what else to do, he ran over and opened one of the closets. Inside he found a stiffly pressed, well-decorated uniform that obviously belonged to a very important general. He liked the strength of its appearance. Perhaps this was his costume. Quickly he dressed himself and stood at attention in front of one of the large dressing mirrors. His heart sank. This was a bold wardrobe indeed . . . but not his. As much as he didn't want to, he took off the uniform. He tried another closet. This had in it a gaily colored costume from a circus. Not wasting a minute, he jumped into it. No good. Besides not fitting him, the costume made him look and feel like a clown. His desperation mounted. He tried another closet.

This time a statesman. Next closet a bum. On and on he went through the closets. Very little fit right, and if it did, it didn't feel right. He came to the last closet. Should he open it? His heart raced. As he reached for the handle, he felt his head start to spin in tight circles that were drawing him in. He fought to hold on. After all, this closet must be the one holding his costume. It was the only one left. As the door opened, he gasped. The closet was empty. This was too much for him. He sagged to the floor.

When he awoke, it was to the sound of concerned people all around him. There was a nice cool cloth on his forehead. Someone was asking him if he was all right. His head ached slightly. Then, for a split instant, terror gripped him as he remembered looking in vain through all of the closets. Just as quickly, a feeling of deep calm came and washed away the fear.

The calm stayed. He remembered who he was. It all came back to him. Earlier that evening, while making his rounds prior to opening the playhouse, he had slipped in the dressing room and knocked his head. The blow had made him temporarily and painfully forget that *he was the owner of the theater, not one of the characters acting on its stage.*

This story teaches us that anxiety, self-doubt and a host of other despairing inner states rush into the spotlight and take over the stage when we live without the knowledge of our True Nature and our True Identity. Once this high self-understanding is restored to us, the painful problems that are caused by its absence effortlessly disappear. Nervous fears about ourself are replaced with calm self-command.

The Strange Non-Life of the False Self

A man who doesn't know his true identity does not know that he doesn't really know. The fact that he is confused, frightened and still searching for himself remains almost totally unsuspected by him, because he has unknowingly assumed a false identity.

This temporary, false self *feels* real because it is animated and driven along by the man's reactions as he seeks himself. The fact that this lower nature is driven does not mean it is alive. A bulldozer rolls along too, but it cannot see or understand why it smashes into things. It is a machine. So, in many ways, is the false self.

The false self is fueled by negative emotional reactions which, in turn, are maintained by habitual incorrect thinking. Because these punishing thoughts and emotions are merely the mechanical movements of our lower nature, they are in *time*. This means they have no choice but to fade with the events that gave them birth. As these negative feelings slowly lose their force, so too does the false life of the false self they had once animated.

Fearing the death of itself because the temporary reactions that gave it life are now fading, the false self is then compelled to start its strange non-life cycle all over again. It begins to crave and to seek out new, more intense excitements or troubles; and when it can't find any, it creates what it needs to sustain itself until conditions become more favorable. For instance, the false self loves to pick fights with others because whether *you* win or lose is of no consequence to it. Your distress is its life's blood, and so all it needs to do in order to win is to keep you fighting. As a matter of fact, the false self is the master of making mountains out of molehills, because it loves nothing better than dark and bumpy downhill roads. Our unhappy part in this recurring nightmare is that we willingly go along on this dark drive that leads us to repetitious events and unhappy endings. Why? Because we have mistakenly assumed this false identity that lives for troubles and we fear that the end of its existence means the end of ours. Nothing could be further from the truth.

Of course, the real problem is that our present life-level can't tell the difference between a ride to Dracula's castle and a trip to Disneyland, and so it tells us that we have no choice but to cave in to the demands of the false self. This one point alone is all the reason in the world to dedicate your days to raising your life-level. If this fact doesn't convince you to go to work, then let this next idea inspire you to new and higher actions. Thinking that the end of this nervous nature is the end of who you really are is, as Vernon Howard so beautifully writes, like thinking that the end of the storm means the end of the sky.

The sky is forever. And so is your True Nature.

Start Seeing Through the Blame Game

Wouldn't you agree that no real friend of yours would ever want you to hurt yourself? And wouldn't you also agree that if you did have a trusted friend that you later found out had lied to you, you wouldn't trust him again — at least not the third, fourth or fifth time? You know the saying: Fool me once, shame on you. Fool me twice, shame on me! For the sake of our studies, let me add one more line to this popular old saying: Fool me over and over again and I obviously don't recognize a foolish idea when I hear one! And that's just the point.

We are being fooled almost moment to moment by habitual thoughts and feelings that *we have stopped listening to*. This amazing insight offers us a good explanation why we end up as often as we do in those painful situations, in which the last words usually spoken go something like, "How in the world did I get myself into this mess?" Sound familiar? It should. And while the answer to this woeful question should rescue us from similar future sticky situations, it rarely works out that way. This is very important to admit to ourselves. The truth is we keep falling into the same old snares. Why?

There is an authentic answer to this question that may surprise you. The reason we haven't as yet realized Real Rescue — and so usually wind up trapped in a tangle once more — is because every time we ask ourselves how we've managed to get stuck again, we usually turn right around and tell ourselves the answer. And so the sad cycle starts all over. It doesn't have to go this way. With a little closer examination and the help of a few Higher Ideas, we can see that we couldn't have possibly come up with the "answer" that we did. Why? Listen to this new and true explanation as to why we seem to keep repeating the same mistakes in our lives: If we *really* knew the answer to that recurring problem of ours, we wouldn't have had it in the first place!

"I know that I have misled myself before, but this is amazing. If I haven't been giving myself these misleading answers, then where are they coming from?"

"All angular answers come from the false self."

"But why? I mean, what could be its motive? Why the deception?"

"It wants you to assume its position."

"And what is that?"

"Look closely and you'll see that the answers you are always given as to why you are unhappy are that someone or something outside of you is making you feel that way."

"What's wrong with that answer?"

"Everything. There is no profit in blaming your painful position in life on other people or an uncaring world. This is the solution the false self wants you to swallow, because it knows that if it can get you to see life its way, then you will have no choice but to spend the rest of your life struggling with life. This is its conquest. First it blows you off course and then it gets you to blame ill winds. Its very existence depends on keeping you off balance and looking in the wrong direction."

Start seeing through the blame game by learning to let go of all the familiar but self-abandoning answers the false self wants you to believe in. Own your own life. Use the following special exercise for Higher Self-Recovery.

For True Self–Command Just Stop, Look and Listen

If he could get away with it, the just-captured thief would eagerly point his trembling finger at a man running down the street and exclaim, "There goes the real culprit!" This is exactly the way in which the internal crimes of the false self go on unchecked. This is why, if we ever want to arrest this inner thief of real life, we must learn to STOP, LOOK and LISTEN. This inner exercise for true self-command is guaranteed to shut down the covert answers and operation of the false self.

The next time that you are feeling anxious — or afraid or worried about a problem you are facing — before you do anything: STOP, LOOK and LISTEN. Remember that the false self is never far away when you are feeling bad. It knows that once it can get you running in the direction of its choice, sheer momentum will do the rest of its work. That is why you come to a *STOP* first. Defy the inner shouts that are trying to spur you on. Don't give them any authority. They are just noises; bad ones at that. Treat them as such.

Then *LOOK*. But be sure to look in the right direction. This is critical. *Look at what is talking to you, not where it is pointing*. This way you won't ever be fooled again and sent on another wild goose chase. So take a real good look. If it is an anxious or unhappy feeling that you are looking at, quietly determine from your own understanding that no negative state is interested in ending itself. This will help you to take the third and last step.

Now *LISTEN*. If you have done the first two steps correctly, you will soon witness the false self start having a fit. Let it rage. *That is all it can do*. It has no power. Its only strength was in your past ignorance of just how truly powerless it was. Just remain right there, inwardly alert and attentive. Your work is done. In the past you might have let these deceptive dark feelings guide you, but now you see through their tricks. In time their roar will dwindle to a whimper and then completely disappear.

You now know that for the first time in your life you have won a true victory for yourself. At last you have deposited something of true value in the most important bank of all — the bank of your own understanding. And believe me, this account pays interest of the Highest kind.

And what about that nagging personal problem? To your great relief, you will discover that it wasn't at all what the false self was trying to make you believe. The problem you are left to solve, assuming one still exists after this lying, lower nature has been thrown out, doesn't even resemble the fearsome giant that had been stalking you earlier. The false self can throw terrifying shadows, but now you can cast Inner Light. There is no contest.

Let Go and Realize Real Rescue

Doesn't this make perfect sense? If we need to be rescued from something, then whatever is rescuing us can't be part of what it rescues us from. Said in a different way, you don't jump on a tiger's back to escape a lion. A terrified rabbit running from a fox only thinks he finds safety when a coyote offers him shelter. This shows us that any desperate attempt to escape a trouble usually leads us right back into more trouble.

So it should be clear to us at this point that Real Rescue from our problems can only come to us from above the level of our problem. And yet, we have also discovered that in order for any solution to be real, it must be found somewhere *within* us, since that is the real location of our problems. The question then becomes: How can we reconcile these two seemingly separate and distant notions: rescue from *above* and solution from *within*? The answer may surprise you. *Above* and *within* mean the exact same thing when it comes to attracting Higher Help.

We can call this new and Higher location of Real Rescue the True Self or Higher Nature. If you prefer, call it God, Truth or Reality. The name doesn't matter, because it isn't what we call this force for self-rescue that gives it authority over our painful conditions. Its power is its elevated position, which is above and outside of the false self's sphere of influence. This beneficent and Real Intelligence becomes your intelligence whenever you refrain from attempting to rescue yourself long enough for it to show you that what you need is more *understanding*, not more battle plans. Temporarily abandoning yourself in this special way, where you consciously watch and so suspend the influences and activities of the false self by refusing to go along with its directives, allows Authentic Understanding to flow into the vacancy and give you real direction.

Everyone knows that a good general carefully chooses where he will engage the enemy. In this way he always has the advantage of the upper ground. The same principle holds true in our work when it comes to learning to let go of who we are *not*.

In our battle with the false self, we defeat it not by running away or through struggle with it, but by standing still long enough to see that we have mistakenly attributed power to it.

One day it will be your greatest pleasure to realize that this false nature has no real power to pain you, outside of what you give to it through your wrong reactions. This important concept always raises lots of questions in my classes. Lets review a particularly helpful illustration I recently gave to one student. Jack said he could feel the vice-like grip of anxious thoughts and feelings even in his sleep. He wanted more insight. "How is it possible, according to Higher Principles, that stormy emotions could feel at once so pervasive and strong; yet be powerless?" Here is how we resolved this seeming contradiction and helped Jack to start realizing Real Rescue.

Two Worlds, Two Natures, Two Selves

The scorching heat in the southwestern desert regions can be phenomenal. It has been known to explode rocks, carve the earth, and create thermal lifts that reach tens of thousands of feet into the air. These giant thermal currents can throw a jumbo passenger jet around like a leaf in the wind. This is definite power. All creatures who inhabit this mostly waterless domain either live by its laws or perish.

But just slightly west and north of the great deserts — in fact, overlooking these barren lands — are majestic green and snow-capped mountains. No waves of heat lash these lofty regions and disturb their ages-long quiet sovereignty. Here you will always find an abundance of mouth-chilling fresh water.

What point am I painting? The uncontested punishing power of the desert is not even a whisper on these high slopes. The desert's power is no power in the mountains. Why? Because the desert's nature doesn't exist for the mountain.

While it's geographically true that the desert and the mountain are often found next to each other, they really have nothing in common. They have completely different natures. Here lies an interesting idea. Let's follow it and see where it goes. I'm certain it will lead us up.

We understand that the valley heat can't reach the peaks. The mountain dwellers stay cool. But, from time to time, the cold and sparkling waters from the snow melt do reach the desert floor. The life there is enriched by this seasonal abundance. In fact, in many cases, life in the desert depends greatly upon this sweet downward flow. We can summarize all of this as follows: The mountain's higher nature can reach down into the desert and bring it life, but the desert's lower nature has no effect on the mountains.

We will always want to remember this natural relationship, for it reveals to us much more than just the play of forces that move the world around us. This important illustration also tells about the worlds within us and how nothing can stand in the way of our eventually attaining the higher, happier life. Here's why.

Like the mountain and the desert, we too have two separate natures that live in two totally different worlds. These inner natures are called True Self and the false self. We've already learned enough about the false self to be able to see the parallels between its nature and that of the desert's. The false self is nothing but a strange series of temporary shapes built up out of the ceaselessly shifting sands of our own doubt-filled thoughts and feelings. This windswept and self-stinging lower nature knows *nothing* outside of itself. It doesn't know anything about the majesty of the Mountain — of True Self. It can't. Just as a summer insect can't know anything about ice, the false self is bound to remain in its realm. The only power it possesses is over those things that are by their nature resigned to remain in its domain.

The more fully we can see Truth's dynamics at play in either the outer or inner worlds, the more we are encouraged and strengthened in our resolve to walk away from this desert-like nature and to begin the climb toward our Sovereign, True Self. Our new courage isn't really a force which we can call our own — it comes to us out of our steadily growing realization that the "powers" of the false self are strictly limited to the world it inhabits. Of what concern is the desert sandstorm to the high mountain pine? Absolutely none! So there it is. There is nothing real to stop us from rising.

Use the Special Insights in this chapter review to start quietly rising above yourself.

1. *The only power the false self has* over *us is that we enjoy living* under *it.*

2. *The more the false self can clash with reality, the more alive it feels.*

3. *The difference between* feeling *like someone and* being *someone is the difference between a desert and a mountaintop life.*

4. *Realize new heights by refusing to live lower.*

5. *The false self loves to build on shifting sands and then complain that life sinks.*

6. *Your real Mountain Home, your True Nature, doesn't have any wish or need to feel high. It* is *High.*

7. *Feeling like someone special because others or events have lifted you is like living in a sandcastle that was built for you at water's edge.*

8, *Losing is the false self's idea of winning, which is why it looks forward to fighting with reality every day.*

9. *The false self is* nothing *that feels like* something; *the false self is* no one *that feels like* someone.

10. *Treasure what is True and one day what is True will reveal its Mountaintop Treasure to you.*

CHAPTER 3

How to Defeat What's Defeating You

The biggest problem facing us as individuals is that we have all been caught up in the race of looking for relief. Our time would be spent far more profitably looking for strength. When caught in a fierce storm, why scramble to find a cave at the foot of the mountain when the same energy can be used to climb? There is a choice. You can tremble within the cave, or live above the tempests that lash the valley below. Our mistake is that we are trying to figure out how to cope with suffering — make the best of it — instead of learning how to terminate it. We would never tolerate a dictatorial government, so why do we put up with all of the inner-tyrants, including their leader, the chief dictator, better known as the false self? We need not. A revolt is necessary, and I can promise you that victory is assured. However, you must revolt intelligently. Don't waste your time planning a coup in the workplace or at home. Leave your relationships alone. They are not the problem. If you want to live the ever-pleasant, ever-present life, the only regime you must overthrow is your present way of thinking. As you will soon see, this is not nearly as difficult as it may sound.

The first step in this right rebellion to reclaim your own life is to learn what it means to think *about* yourself instead of *from* yourself. The difference being that when you learn to think about your thinking, this special kind of self-separation allows you to question its intelligence. This is a highly intelligent act because thinking *from* yourself lets unexamined thoughts race by and into action. For instance, saying yes when you mean to say no, or vice versa, is a small but painful illustration of what happens to us when we don't examine our thoughts and feelings before speaking. Resentment almost always follows. And, as we are learning, one of the chief tricks of the false self is to make you think that what *it* wants is what you want.

In this case, the false self loves to feel resentful. Resenting someone is like a pleasure cruise on a luxury liner for this shallow nature, because it can crash and sink itself again and again over the situation. A situation, incidentally, it caused itself but whose wreckage you are left to clean up. So you see it can be highly profitable to challenge your own thinking. Just as you would never buy a sack of diamonds without first confirming the seller's professional standing and the stones' actual value, you should never buy any of your own thoughts or feelings until you are certain of their source and that they are indeed yours! Don't be surprised by this idea. I'll show you one example of how we think we are thinking while actually the thinking we are calling ours can be proven counterfeit and worse than valueless.

Snap Yourself Out of Psychic Slumber

I'm sure that we can all agree that no intelligent, conscious man or woman would ever intentionally hurt him or herself. It is important that we are in agreement about this precept. No one would choose to ache. Yet the fact remains that all of us do hurt ourselves every day with bursts of anger or fits of depression or anxiety. There can be no doubt, beginning with the physical level and on up, that fear and worry exact a definite toll on all levels of our health and well-being. Intelligent, conscious beings would never intentionally hurt themselves, but we somehow manage to do just that in one way or another almost every day. So how do we reconcile this contradiction? There is only one possible conclusion that we can draw from these facts, and it is imperative that we paint this picture clearly to ourselves.

We must be unconscious while *thinking* that we are awake! In other words, during those times of self-betrayal when we are hurting ourselves or others with negative inner states, even though our eyes are open and all kinds of sensations are coursing through us, we must be asleep to what we are doing to ourselves or we wouldn't be doing it. Somehow, and we will discover just exactly how, we have become separated from the real Intelligence within us that knows better than to punish itself. There is never, I repeat, never *any* intelligent reason to feel bad. If you will only let these truthful ideas prove this astonishing fact to you, one day this new understanding will go before you and defeat all that has been defeating you.

Now comes an important moment in our self-questioning. This is what we have been working towards. We are about to win the prize that always follows when we persist with our inner lessons. If *real* Intelligence is incapable of hurting itself, then how can we call *any* thinking that leads to a stressful state intelligent? Obviously we can no longer continue to call such thinking intelligent unless we want to go on sinking from this present level of thinking.

Let's review briefly. Intelligence does not cause itself to suffer. Yet, as proven, we suffer. This can only mean that a counterfeit intelligence has been passed off on us and its thinking accepted as our very own. There is only one way that such a sinister switch could take place within us and go undetected. During those all-too-familiar worry-packed moments, we are asleep to ourselves. In this strange psychic slumber we only dream we are awake, so can you see the solution to this sorry state? Since unawareness of ourselves is the only problem, then awareness is the only answer. A sting operation can only work as long as the victim believes that one of the players who is secretly in on the sting is trying to help him. Let's say all of this in another way.

You may not be able to *think* your way out, but you can *see* your way clear. This special kind of inner seeing is safety. Waking up to yourself is the same as letting go of all those self-defeating thoughts and feelings that have been telling you how to win.

How to Break Free of Unhappy Thoughts and Feelings

"All of this is starting to make sense, but even so, how can just *seeing* something like wrong thoughts or feelings within me free me of their influence? They feel so strong!"

"Your feelings, good or bad, are not the masters of your life; they are merely moments within it."

"Again, that makes sense, but how does that help me break their painful hold on me?"

"You break free of unhappy thoughts and emotions by seeing that, even though it may feel that way at the moment, you are not owned by them. You are only temporarily occupied. Seeing this important difference instantly changes your attitude toward any stressful character that attempts to intimidate you into giving it authority over your life. Remember what we have discussed. Real Intelligence has no authority outside of its own nature. As you come to own yourself, which is the sole purpose of this life, it becomes impossible to ever think or feel that you are owned by anything or anyone else. This is the only true strength."

It is an ironclad guarantee that these ideas, coupled with persistent self-investigation, will gradually reveal to you that the false self is nothing more than a shadow that can throw its voice. Its main job is to see that your troubles always appear to be everything and everywhere but what and where they really are. The only thing special about the false self is its wide range of special effects. The following illustration will help us to better understand these exciting and self-liberating ideas.

Do you remember *The Wizard of Oz* and how in their first meetings with the Wizard, Dorothy and her lovable friends were so terrified? Each time the Wizard spoke, his voice rolled through the grand hall like thunder! And how it appeared to the small band of friends, as they stood there shaking, that this mighty wizard had the power to hurl around spears of flame and smoke? To them he seemed like a mighty being, maybe even a god. That is until Toto, Dorothy's little dog, pulled back a certain curtain which exposed a strange little man standing at an elaborate control panel. Whoever this man was, he was very busy pushing buttons and pulling on levers and talking a mile a minute into a microphone. At the same instant that he would push a button or pull a lever, flames or smoke would billow through the hall. And each time he spoke in his tiny voice into the microphone, the hall would be filled with the roar of the Wizard's voice shouting out the exact same words. Suddenly it was obvious to Dorothy that the great "Wizard" was in reality just a projection of the little man hiding behind the curtain.

In fact, this little man was so involved with his act that he didn't know his hiding place had been discovered until Dorothy sternly told him to stop his performance. But even as Dorothy stood there, shocked at the cruel trick that had been played on her, she realized *in the same instant* that there was no more reason to be scared and troubled. The show was over! It was in the seeing that there came the freeing.

You'll experience the same welcome relief when you reach up and pull back the mental curtain held so desperately in place by the false self.

Give Your Life Story a Happy Ending

We have all seen those incredible scenes in the movies in which the ship is on fire and sinking, women and children are crying, and there is always one man who had earlier secreted aboard a small treasure of gold and jewels and is not about to give it up. So he runs back to his cabin, stuffs all the jewels and coins he can into his pockets, puts the heavy gold chains around his neck and then, because he was delayed in getting to the life rafts, he is forced to jump into the water, where he immediately sinks like the stone he has made of himself!

This story illustrates a classic example of a man defeating himself. Of course, that's the movies and he may even have deserved his watery fate; still, no one consciously chooses to lose, especially his own life.

When we watch a scene like this, we ask ourselves "how could anyone be so stupid?" After all, we reason from the safety and warmth of our own living room sofas, what is more important to someone on a sinking ship—a life raft full of air or a jacket full of heavy gold and silver coins? We would never make such a mistake, right? Let's see if our self-certainty can stand the light of our honest self-investigation. What about those daily life-wrecks of anxiety, depression and anger where we find ourselves sinking beneath waves of unhappy thoughts and feelings? Why is it that after a collision with an unwanted event we go down so easily? You may be surprised to discover that the exact same forces working against the man in our story are working against you. However, as you are also about to discover, you possess a power far greater than any of these self-wrecking forces will ever wield. Once you assume command of this powerful principle, you will see that no inner-storms or stressful conditions can ever again run you aground. Let's go back now and give this new power to the man in our shipwreck and see how it changes the end of the story and his life.

We'll pick up the story again just as he has abandoned himself and starts running back toward his cabin to collect his treasure. The diffused red glow of the emergency lamps and the thickening smoke make it almost impossible to see the numbers on the doors. His terror and desperation mount with every passing second. Suddenly, the heavy anguish lifts from his face. He deliberately and calmly turns and heads for the life rafts with the rest of the passengers and leaves his fortune to go down with the ship. What happened? What could have so drastically changed the ending of our story? What benevolent force could have come in and so moved the man to save himself when he was bent on an action that would have cost him his life?

At that crucial moment, while he was in the very process of making all the wrong choices, the man in our story *woke up*. Suddenly he could see himself and exactly where he was. This rescuing awareness instantly provided him with the understanding of his perilous situation and gave him an immediate and intelligent course of action to be taken. To his further amazement, part of that rescuing heightened awareness of himself included the shock of seeing that his own thoughts had actually blinded him. His *thoughts* cared nothing for him; only for what they wanted! This higher glimpse, happening all at once, helped him to abandon himself so that he could in turn safely abandon the sinking ship. He lived to have another day and perhaps another fortune.

This new and happier ending to our story gives us our first glimpse of a new and indispensable tool for authentic self-rescue. This powerful principle and higher self-action is called self-observation.

Higher Awareness Through Self–Observation

Do you remember when we discussed the ideas about real intelligence and how an awake, conscious man would never intentionally hurt himself? Self-observation is how we learn to remain inwardly vigilant. It is how we stay awake to our thoughts and feelings even as they are coursing through us. When we can observe ourselves in this new way, we allow our natural higher intelligence, our Higher Nature, to prevail over the unnatural thoughts and feelings of our self-defeating lower nature.

Self-observation allows you to understand what you are witnessing within you instead of being dominated or devastated by it, because your new and higher inner-position as the observer is outside of and so separate from what it is watching. This unique inner-sanctuary must always make the right choices, because it has no past investment in any events or their possible outcome, so it is *free* to select what is *intelligent*. Intelligence cannot be bound by the momentum of accumulated desires. The silent observer does not think. He *sees*. This is an important point. To self-observe means that you cannot be self-absorbed. Higher awareness through self-observation increases your field of choices, because this elevated inner-position places you high above the game and lets you see all of the players. On the other hand, self-absorption is like being on the field. Not only can't you see all of the players, but those that you can see are more often than not slamming into you, turning you around and around until you don't know which way to run. That's the whole point: Stop running and bumping, and start seeing.

There is no greater power for self-change than self-observation because this new inner-vision alone can provide you with true self-knowledge. Being self-liberated is the same as living fully from your Higher Nature. In this lofty state you enjoy the freedom that comes with having let go of your false self. This Higher Nature rests above you. Join it. Let it guide you all the way back to your true home within yourself.

As you persist each day with this important and practical task of adding more inner light to yourself — of making it your aim to stay up in the grandstand and out of the brawls on the field — you may find yourself becoming increasingly disturbed by some of the negativities you are seeing within yourself down on the field. This is a good indication that you are making real progress. You must apply the principles you have learned even to this new kind of disturbance. This uproar you are experiencing is the false self trying its best to get you into the free-for-all down on the field. Stay in the stands in your observation post. Don't be concerned with anything you may see. Remember, light need never fear any shadow, and anything you may discover within you that is frightening comes from the shadow world. Your only task is to turn up the light. It will take care of the rest.

Let's review this kingly principle. To see yourself in this new way means that at the same moment of being aware of your physical self, you are also watching what you are thinking and feeling without involving your old inclinations to jump in and judge. Simply stated, self-observation is a way of being fully aware of yourself while remaining free from any self-concern. In this unique psychological posture you remain effortlessly apart from all wrong concerns because, should any of them arise, they are treated as just something else you are seeing, not as something you are.

At first, this idea of expanded self-awareness may sound to you like a little too much going on all at once. I assure you that it is not. Once you get the feel for it, self-observation is not any more difficult than leisurely watching a juggler under the Big Top. He may have as many as six or seven assorted objects flipping and spinning all at once, but that is of *no concern to you*. Seeing takes no effort. You are just enjoying the performance! And while we're speaking of performances, you will be happy to know that nothing brings the curtain down faster on the false self than this special kind of inner attention. You will see that self-observation is to our lower nature what sunlight is to a cave-dwelling bat. Just as the bat cannot stand the sun's bright rays, neither can the false self live in the light of this new and self-healing awareness.

Inner Work Rewards the Inner You

What we must always remember is that the only work we do of lasting value is the work that we do for ourselves within ourselves. We have a definite conditioned dependency to think of things as worthwhile only if someone else recognizes their value. This painful kind of thinking not only leaves us trying to please others, but it also discourages us from embarking upon the exciting journey of self-investigation.

In our appearance-oriented thinking, we wrongly believe that unless someone else can see our inner efforts or in some way approve our self-discoveries, our work has been in vain. Nothing could be further from the truth. Inner work rewards the Inner You. This is your true and Higher Nature. Ever-present but as yet unrealized, your Higher Nature is pleasing to itself and so needs nothing outside of its own elevated state in order to feel successful. This exalted inner condition, which is the source of true self-liberation, already lives within you. It is not something that you need to add to yourself, since it has always belonged to you. This special knowledge teaches us that this Great Prize is a realization and not an acquisition.

"So if you can't give yourself this Inner Victory, how do you win?"

"You must learn to stop thinking in terms of beginnings and endings, successes and failures; and begin to treat everything in your life as a *learning* experience instead of a *proving* one."

"How will this help me to realize my true Successful Self?"

"When approaching life in this new way, you will no longer waste your precious energies endlessly battling to prove yourself to yourself and others. Now your energies can be put to much higher use, which will initially enable you to clearly see how you have been stubbornly clinging to self-defeating ideas and beliefs."

"That doesn't sound like something I'm going to be interested in seeing!"

"The highest peaks of great mountains almost always have banks of dark clouds resting just beneath them. You must climb through these clouds in order to conquer the heights. Then the higher view belongs to you."

"I'm afraid I won't be strong enough."

"You don't need to be strong, only willing to see. If you will do your part, which is to reveal you to yourself, your Higher Nature will provide you with all the strength you need. It is this new strength that allows you to let go of the self-limiting and fear-producing thoughts and feelings which have been darkening your life and holding you down. Having dropped the unnatural heaviness from your spirit, you now naturally begin to rise. The higher you go, the easier flows your New Life. Now the only direction you want to go in life is up!"

Self-Correction Is Self-Elevation

We are a peculiar race of beings. On one hand, each of us professes to be concerned with growing and self-developing while, on the other hand, none of us ever wants to be wrong. This is a paralyzing contradiction. If we are always right, or at least afraid of being wrong, what have we to learn? Couched in our hidden attitude is the belief that we already know everything.

This is a serious problem if we are at all serious in our quest for self-liberation, since this Higher Freedom comes to us in direct proportion to what we are willing to learn about ourselves.

Learning is a correction process. Real correction, at any level, always purifies the matter and so leaves it less confused and thus in a higher state. Taking this beautiful idea one step further reveals to us the promise that self-elevation always follows self-correction. You may not as yet fully understand the implications of this powerful Inner Law, but it holds within it the promise of endless heights.

The whole idea of modifying ourselves, of slowly improving through time, is born out of our reluctance to be wrong. Perhaps this is why so few of us ever really learn to stop hurting ourselves. Let's take a moment and look at the difference between self-improvement and self-correction. With self-improvement we teach ourselves lessons of our choice based on what we think we need to learn in order to grow. Self-improvement teaches and confirms the process of self-addition, in which we acquire new knowledge, behaviors and beliefs.

With self-correction we *learn* for ourselves that we have been teaching ourselves incorrectly. Seeing this allows us to let go of our incorrect thinking. As we experience the benefits of letting go of ourselves, vigorous new inner growth then takes place as naturally as it does for a young plant that has been moved from a shadowy place out into the sunlight. A new tree cannot grow in the shadow of an old one. Learning can only take place outside the shadow of pride. Anything that resists correction is a part of what is wrong.

While we are on the subject of resistance, we should recognize that pride is the middle name of the false self. It is this false nature of ours that always leaps to defend itself when confronted with any kind of meaningful correction. Remember, this lower nature is happy with its current disorderly existence. You lose when it wins and it wins by getting you to deny or protect your mistake. Denying any problem makes you its guardian and leaves you chained to being wrong.

Let's go over these important principles once more. Being wrong is not the problem. Defending the life-level that produced the wrongness is where we make the mistake. Once we start denying or defending the problem, we have turned it from what should have been only a temporary condition into a permanent state. You are not tied to any past mistake unless you lash yourself to it. This is exactly what the false self wants you to do. It does this by convincing you that *you* are wrong. Once it has accomplished this, it can continue selling you anchors that look like life vests. Let's name a few of these inner weights that we mistakenly cling to in a storm.

Guilt and anxiety are two of the false self's favorite deceptions. It knows that all it needs to do in order to win another day for itself is to get you started desperately seeking solutions for your problem or busy pretending to yourself and others that you don't have one. Either way, it's got you right where it wants you because now you *believe* that the problem is yours. There may indeed be something wrong, but no matter how it may feel or appear, all personal difficulties are born out of a lack of understanding. By trying to hide the problem from yourself, you shut the window on the possibility of looking into your current life-level, which is the only world where real correction can take place. This is why we must never hide anything from ourselves. Remember, once the problem is out of sight, so is the only possible solution.

Here are four Higher Guidelines for realizing Real Solutions:

1

If your intention is to go higher, then the detection of what is wrong within you is the correction.

2

If you see *you are wrong, then at that instant you can give up* being *wrong.*

3

Giving up the painful temporary identity of being wrong is the same as letting go of your lower nature, the false self.

4

Rightness has never betrayed you. Self-deception is self-betrayal.

Here is one last special idea for us to mentally return to again and again: If we will place learning before our pleasure, one day learning will come before our pain.

The Power that Defeats Defeat

You possess a potential power that is superior to any difficulty that life may ever present. This immense inner capability enables anyone who will claim it to instantly rise above his challenger. It makes no difference what form the challenge may assume or how huge it looms. This latent power of yours can render it harmless and ultimately make it disappear.

This friendly force that can turn your life into a series of victories is *the power to question defeat*. Now, before you start insisting that you already question your stresses and strains, allow me to show you the difference between right *intention* and right *direction*. A little story will help illustrate this higher idea.

A happy traveler noticed a tired-looking man seated off to the side of a small but pleasant country road. It appeared that even the cool shade of the tree seemed to weigh upon him. The traveler asked if he might sit for awhile and refresh himself. It wasn't long after they had shared some bread, an apple, and sparse, polite conversation that the obviously unhappy man spoke up. He begged his new companion's forgiveness and went on to ask if the traveler could help him.

It seemed he had been wandering for weeks, going through all kinds of difficulties; but for all his intense effort, he could tell he wasn't getting any closer to his destination. He wanted to return to the home of his childhood. The traveler understood his plight and asked where was this home. The man, showing his first smile, called out the name of the small town where he had been born. The traveler looked at him gently and then spoke. "I know how it feels to want to go home; but *along with your right intention, you've got to have the right direction.* You've been headed the wrong way, friend."

The kind traveler then pointed him in the right direction and the wandering man soon made it back to the home of his youth.

Let's look at this story through the eyes of our new understanding so we, too, can make it back to our inner home, our true Higher Nature. So far we have learned that our stressful, pain-filled experiences are not caused by people or events, but by our *reactions* to them. And yet, if we will honestly examine the way we presently question our defeats, we will see that we are still desperately seeking answers that serve only to correct the surface or exterior conditions. We are still blaming circumstances for crushing us. The direction of our questions proves that we are still thinking incorrectly toward our problems. This is supremely important to grasp if we wish to change our inner and outer world. By their very nature our old questions tend to make and then keep us victims, because these questions imply that someone or something outside of ourselves is punishing us. No human being is a victim of any punishment outside of his own undeveloped life-level from which his inner reactions are seen as outer attacks. This is why we must learn to turn our questions into tools for developing self-wholeness instead of letting them lead us off in the wrong direction. As a matter of fact, there should be a new question forming in your mind just about now. If you will, let me help you formulate it, because this question *is* pointed in the right direction. It goes something like this:

"Where in the world did I get all of those wrong questions that have kept me the victim and at odds with the world?"

"I'll let you answer this right question for yourself. Based on what we've discovered so far, who stands to gain the most from keeping you fighting with shadows and grasping at straws?"

"The false self!"

"That's right. This false nature always divides in order to conquer. From this moment forward, we are going to learn to ask our own questions—questions that address and illuminate what it is *within* us that always feels as though it is being punished."

These new questions are the power that defeats defeat. They alone insure total victory. Each time you ask the *right* question about an inner ache, the very nature of your question places you safely outside the tricky influences of your lower nature that can only exist by turning you into an avenging victim.

Here are ten new questions that lead to self-wholeness. Use them to see the difference between how you used to think and how you will question defeat from now on. You will win!

Questions for Self-Wholeness

1

Instead of always asking yourself "Why do these things always happen to me?"

Learn to ask: *What is it inside of me that attracts these painful situations?*

2

Instead of always asking yourself why things had to go this way or be that way...

Learn to ask: *Why is the way I feel always determined by external conditions?*

3

Instead of always asking yourself how to protect yourself in challenging situations...

Learn to ask: *What is it in me that always needs to be defended?*

4

Instead of always asking yourself how to clear up your mental fog...

Learn to ask: *Can confusion know anything about clarity?*

5

Instead of always asking yourself what to do about tomorrow (or the next minute)...

Learn to ask: *Can there ever be intelligence in anxiety or worry?*

6

Instead of always asking yourself why does so-and-so act this or that way...

Learn to ask: *What's inside of me that wants to hurt itself over how anyone acts?*

7

Instead of always crying out, "Why me?"

Learn to ask: *Who is this "me" that always feels this way?*

8

Instead of always asking yourself if you've made the right choice...

Learn to ask: *Can fear ever make a safe decision?*

9

Instead of always asking yourself why doesn't so-and-so see how wrong they are...

Learn to ask: *Is what I'm feeling about that person right now good for me? Or them?*

10

Instead of always asking yourself how to get others to approve you...

Learn to ask: *What do I really want, the applause of the crowds or to quietly have my own life?*

Put Yourself in the Driver's Seat

As she boarded the luxurious tour bus, Jessica couldn't believe that she was actually taking a day off for herself. It was hard to imagine that a full six months had flown by since she accepted her new position and had moved to this small coastal city. She knew she was going to enjoy what the travel brochure had promised would be a pampered and casual day of scenic wonders. The tour was expensive, but she had earned her pleasure and she was going to have it. She sat on the edge of her seat as the bus pulled out of the depot.

Twenty minutes later, over the oohs and aahs of the other twenty-five passengers, the driver was describing the natural wonders of the breathtaking blue-and-green seascape that spread endlessly beneath them. The promise of a beautiful day sent a wave of pleasure through her, and she relaxed in her tufted seat. Just then, one of the passengers in front of her jumped out of his seat, walked up to the driver and said he wanted to drive for awhile. The driver stood up, the passenger sat down, and the bus jerked forward. To Jessica's amazement no one around her, including the driver, seemed to mind this odd exchange.

In less than a heartbeat, the beautiful ocean vista had vanished and now all she was looking at outside her window were old, abandoned buildings and trash-littered streets. The new driver was taking the bus through the slums. No one else aboard looked at all surprised, and so she tried her best to relax. The thought came that maybe this was part of the tour, but she didn't remember reading about it. Her thoughts were interrupted when yet another passenger scrambled up to the driver's seat and took over the wheel. Now the bus was racing up and down steep, bumpy streets and over dangerous narrow bridges. Something was definitely wrong. Too numb to speak out and too frightened to move, she sank deeper into her chair as one by one each of the passengers took over the wheel and drove the bus wherever they wanted. Her pleasure cruise had turned into a tunnel of horrors.

She had almost resigned herself to a desperate kind of helpless rage when all of a sudden, from deep within her growing confusion, a thought came that shocked her awake and into a new sense of herself she had never before experienced.

Terrified but determined she got up, she walked over to the driver's seat, and said in a shaky but firm voice, "Now it's my turn to drive."

To her surprise, the passenger-driver got up and gave her his seat. She sat down, took the wheel, and drove herself home.

This story contains many higher lessons that we are going to need to understand if we wish to make it all the way to the ever-pleasant life. When we don't know where we are going or who is driving, a pleasant present is impossible. The only pleasure we can have on this kind of ride through life comes from dreaming about where we are going. We must dream while others drive because if our eyes were open, we would never tolerate where we were being taken.

Even when we do run into a nice rest stop or a pleasant event, there is no lasting pleasure in it for us because we know that we have no real say in how long we get to remain there. These temporary pleasures are usually a strange blend of anticipation and cynicism which we learn to swallow only because we don't as yet know the taste of real pleasure.

Know the Pleasure of Your True Nature

Real pleasure in this life comes from knowing that you are in command of yourself *now*. We like to tell ourselves that we are at the wheel, but, as we learned at the start of the last chapter section, no one would purposely drive himself through the mud or off a cliff. Whenever we find that we are feeling sorry for ourselves, or angry, or worried and anxious, this is a sure sign that we took the wrong seat and that someone or something else is busy steering us down the wrong road.

At first it is humiliating to see and then admit that you only *thought* you were in the driver's seat. This is a necessary shock if we want to identify exactly what is driving us. However, compare this temporary humiliation which eventually places you in command of yourself to the life without it that closely resembles Toad's Wild Ride at Disneyland.

We live from a bottomless basket of endless wants that drive us everywhere, including crazy! Hoping to find comfort and life-direction in your wants is like trying to find shade under a swarm of stinging flies. While it may be cooler, you also have to keep running. Your pleasure is your pain.

Real pleasure is not the *opposite* of pain, it is the *absence* of it. Think about it. What you really want is to be free of your wants. This Higher want becomes an answerable need the more we realize that we do not have to sit by and submit to anything not of our own choosing. No one chooses to be pulled apart unless his or her idea of happiness is going to pieces.

All of us have known those times when we find all of our wants pulling in one direction — and so we may win what we want. Only now these very wants become our haunts. Too late we realize that we didn't *really* win what we *thought* we had; and now we must learn to live with yet one more "prize" that is more a punishment than it is our pleasure.

Here is the key to the ever-pleasant life. Our wants seem to hold the promise of a brighter, more pleasant future, when the truth is that it is their very nature that is disturbing the present. Everything is pleasant *now*. You wouldn't throw a pebble into a pond to quiet its surface. Left alone, the pond reflects the heavens above it. As we learn to leave ourselves alone, the clearer it becomes that we are happier that way. No one likes a nag, so it's no small wonder we don't like ourselves.

Don't be afraid to tell a persistent want that you are taking over the wheel. Let it holler. As all of these inner passengers start to realize that you intend to drive from now on, they will start to exit the bus. At this point you may notice a weird feeling that seems something like loneliness. Believe me, this is just one of the last wants who doesn't like to be ignored. Stay right there in the driver's seat. Even though it may not feel like it at the moment, you have nothing to lose. This is the truth. Don't worry if you aren't sure where you want to go. Stick with your new inner position, and one day you will be happy to see even that worry was just another of the want haunts. Little by little you will discover that you never really needed to know where to go. Now it's pleasant for you wherever you are because pleasure has become your nature instead of your goal.

CHAPTER 4

Lift Yourself Into a Brand New World

"Does a brand new world really exist?"

"Only if you know where to look."

"What direction should I take?"

"Look to yourself."

Within each of us there is an expansive world of thoughts and feelings whose movements determine how we perceive and experience the world outside of us. While this inner-world of thoughts and feelings may not directly bring us what we see, it does profoundly influence how we see our world of relationships and events. This is one of the deeper aspects of an idea we discussed in an earlier chapter about how the inner determines the outer. In other words, we are seeing the exterior but experiencing the interior. One simple example of how this works is when our heart is heavy or troubled. Whenever we happen to feel this way, everything else around us tends to appear equally dark. But there are far deeper implications to this important insight. With patient self-study, we can turn it into a personal breakthrough of the most freeing kind that can lift us to a brand new world. Let's get started.

All of us have felt, at one time or another, trapped in our own life. During these periods of heightened unhappiness we sit convinced that were it not for this unpleasant person or that unfavorable condition, we would be well on our way to realizing our greater potential, instead of being stuck where we are. Over and over again we plan our escapes, and over and over again we seem to return to the same sad state of feeling caged in or confined. For all of our efforts, nothing really changes. New loves, new jobs, even new homes change only the walls that surround us — not our feelings of being imprisoned. We sense that all we have done is changed cells! We mustn't fight with or in any way fear this shocking conclusion. Why? Because this temporarily disturbing discovery about our actual condition contains a crucial insight. It was *never* that person or circumstance that was blocking our moment in the sun. No! In spite of how things may appear to us, we are never trapped by *where* we are. The trap is always *who* we are. Here is a short summary of this new and unusual self-discovery:

When you run into a personal obstacle, you have not run into an outer condition that is denying you happiness. You have run into your own present life-level.

Your Secret Power of Self-Disconnect

Your level of being is what determines *where* you are at any given moment because your experience is always *who* you are. Let me repeat this. For better or for worse, you experience *who* you are, not *where* you are.

Here are a few more examples to help you see this important idea.

All of us have felt:

1. *Lonely in a crowd.*

2. *Out of place at a family gathering.*

3. *Frightened in a loved one's arms.*
4. *Depressed at a party.*
5. *Crowded even though alone.*

When you hear someone say, "I'm sick and tired of it," what he is really saying without realizing it is that he's sick and tired of suffering from his own lack of understanding. This all becomes clear once we understand that unhappiness does not come *at* us, it comes *from* us. For instance, impatience with our level of understanding is the very level of understanding we are impatient with. The understanding of this spiritual principle allows us to disconnect ourselves from our impatience. Life becomes instantly better. For one thing, the frustration fades. In its place, learning flowers. And the more we inwardly grow, the easier our whole life flows.

This new and higher idea of disconnecting ourselves from whatever we think has us blocked leads to true self-liberation because we have never been trapped by anything outside of our own lack of understanding. This is why even the attempt to disconnect ourselves from our present life-level already belongs to a higher level of understanding.

This new, intelligent action we are calling "self-disconnect" works for you by gradually breaking down the painful circle-of-self that is repeatedly formed by asking the problem for the solution. Barriers begin to crumble and disappear, because you have stopped creating them. In the truest meaning of the words, you are getting out of your own way! Practice self-disconnect as often as you can. The more you work at this special kind of letting go, the freer your days will flow and the higher your life will go.

Persistence is everything in your personal work. You must persist even if it is only with your wish to be persistent. You must persist in spite of all forces that seem to be against your wish to break through to a New You. Believe me, there are no real obstacles to keep you from making it all the way to a Brand New World. Remember this. With any true inner- growth, the hardest step is always the one you have never taken before. The greater the doubt you will step across, the greater the possibility for walking beyond yourself, because doubt and fear form the perimeter of all self-limiting barriers. Risk only comes into account in the self-limited view of seeing life as a win/lose scenario.

When self-discovery becomes more important than winning, then every situation in life presents you with an opportunity to win in a new way. Every time you step past yourself, you win a little more freedom . . . freedom to take another and yet another step into the great unknown where eventually, with persistence, fear turns into fearlessness, because you have disconnected yourself from yourself.

How to Let Go of Helpless Feelings

Psychological suffering is a waste of life. It is pointless, cruel, and above all deceptive. I say deceptive because psychological suffering is an unnecessary pain that we are presently certain is not only necessary, but actually unavoidable . . . a part of real life. Mental and emotional suffering are not a part of real life. You do not have to live with any tormenting thoughts or feelings no matter how compelling their cries may be to convince you otherwise. There is always a choice when it comes to psychological suffering. You need *never* surrender to any wave of helplessness that leaves you feeling sorry for being alive.

"I want to agree with what you say, but I'm afraid the truth is it doesn't seem to matter what direction I choose — eventually I run right into some kind of conflict or unhappiness."

"That's right."

"But I thought you said there was a choice."

"There is, but only when you stop thinking in terms of

choosing ways of escape!"

"Well then, just how should I think towards my suffering?"

"That's just the point. Your suffering is born out of your thinking about yourself in the first place. Any direction or guidance given to you by your thoughts telling you how to break out of your self-confinement is merely the continuation of the very same thoughts that have you feeling imprisoned."

The desperate search for happiness is the continuation of unhappiness. Happiness is never driven to look for itself. It is itself. The drive to become confident is the continuation of self-doubt. The hope for a brighter future is the continuation of a dim and flickering past. Even feeling guilty over getting angry is still the continuation of inner-irritation. Any direction we take to get away from some misery is the continuation of that distress, no matter how much time and space we may put between us and it. As long as we choose from this distressed life-level, our solutions have their roots in the problem. This insight helps us to approach the deeper meaning of Christ's message, "As ye sow, so shall ye reap."

"Yes, the events of my life verify what you are saying. So what do I do? What is my new direction?"

"The problem is your question already assumes you need to *go* somewhere or *do* something. What you need is to stop being the you that you *think* you are."

"But how do I do that?"

"Be willing to see the truth of all that we have been discussing. Start watching yourself in action. Here's just *one* example. Catch yourself listening to a familiar anxious state telling you how to make the best plans for a secure tomorrow — and then ask yourself if it makes sense to ask a shark how to get out of the ocean. Obviously, it doesn't! Catch enough of these cunning conversations in yourself and before too long a real miracle will occur. You'll stop asking yourself for directions because at long last you will no longer believe in the you that's telling you you're lost."

A Technique That Makes Fear Fade

One early evening when he arrived back home from his job at the studio where he worked as a television director, Steven noticed that his young son, Timothy, was sitting outside all alone on the back porch. There wouldn't have been anything so unusual about this except that this was the hour of Tim's favorite TV show. Nothing in the past had ever kept him from this appointed time in front of the television.

Quietly opening the screen door, Steve walked out onto the porch and sat down next to his son. He could see that Timmy was visibly upset over something, and so, putting his arm around him, he asked his son what was wrong. After a few minutes, a sad story emerged. Tim was upset and frightened because at school that day all the children had to get up in front of class and say what they wanted to be when they grew up. Timmy went on to explain that everyone seemed to know who they wanted to be. His pals all gave enthusiastic reports on growing up to become firemen, doctors, or sports players. He was the only in the class who didn't know what he wanted to become, and his classmates teased him about it all day.

A few quiet moments passed and his father looked at him and asked him if he wanted to go somewhere special. Twenty minutes later, Timothy found himself on one of the large sound stages where his father was making his newest movie. The next thing he knew, his dad had lifted him onto the high-back, slick, black chair of one of the cameras and, after throwing a few switches, told him to look into the camera's eye. Tim did as he was told and when he did, he let out a yelp because there was a monster looking right back at him. His father smiled and told him to look again — but this time to keep his eye there no matter how scary it was. Timmy was frightened but he trusted his dad so he did as he was instructed. The monster was still right there and just as terrifying as before, but as he looked through the camera's eye, he felt his father slowly moving the camera back and away from the monster. As the camera and Timmy pulled back, the scene that Timmy was looking at through the camera began to change. At first there was only the monster, but now Timmy was beginning to see more of the set. Funny old windows and velvet curtains, oak tables and chairs, lots of other props filled in the picture that only a moment before had just been the ugly monster.

To his surprise, his father kept rolling the heavy camera back until now he could see all kinds of lights and microphones suspended over the elaborate set where the monster had been. Back further still and now Timothy could see some of the other studio sets and heavily wired ceilings. Way in the distance stood the scary monster.

Timmy knew that his father was teaching him something very important. He already felt a lot better even though he wasn't sure exactly why. On the way home they stopped for a snack and his father explained the lesson to him. Let's listen in.

"Sometimes unpleasant or scary things happen to us, like when you looked into the camera and all you could see was the monster. Whenever this happens, all we can do is think about what we saw and how to get away or protect ourselves from the threat. Like what happened with the monster, you didn't want to look again because you didn't want to see it again. The problem with this choice, Timmy, is that even though you don't look at it again, you are still living in and with the original frightening moment; only now this fear has become a fixed point within you as a memory and you take it wherever you go. Even more amazing is that this unpleasant fixed point within you — this scary memory — is more than likely determining where you go and what choices you make, since you are probably, unknowingly, trying to get away from it."

He paused for a moment to see if his son was taking in the important lesson. Timmy's eyes were sparkling and that was a good sign. He gently continued, "You were out on the back porch when I got home. You were feeling worse and worse the more you tried to make the day's events go away. Trying to make any unpleasant thoughts or feelings go away only fixes them in you. Try to understand this. That's why I made you look at the monster again and again while I kept pulling the camera back. The *wider* the view became in the camera's eye, the less frightening what you were looking at became. Finally, when we pulled all the way back, you could see that there was nothing to be frightened about because you could see the *whole* picture. This is what you must do with every event, every thought and feeling that crosses through your life.

Whenever you feel scared or anxious, remember this important lesson. Mental or emotional suffering takes place only when you have become fixed in the partial. Break your temporary wrong focus and *pull back from yourself.* The wider you can expand your inner-view, the less disturbed you'll be by what you may be seeing."

Timmy looked at his dad and asked, "But what about when I grow up, don't I need to know now what I want to be?"

"Listen carefully, son. The more you could see in the camera's eye, the less frightening everything else became, right?"

"Right, Dad."

"Well, that holds true for who you will want to be as you grow up. There are great possibilities in this life that are going to take time for you to discover. Life will show itself to you, and as it does you'll know just what to do and who to be. There is never any good reason to worry about anything. Treat those kinds of scary feelings just like we did with the monster and pull back; make the scene wider and wider until you see the whole picture. Then you will know there was never anything real to be scared about. Will you try to remember this the next time you feel bad?"

"I'll do my best."

"That's all that's necessary."

Let Go of Loneliness and Discontentment

Nothing is more discontented than our lower nature, the false self. It is always unhappy with one thing or another. If there is one weed in a field of roses, you can bet that is what it will see. Since it has no real life of its own, it must endlessly create stimulating thoughts and feelings of one kind or another in order to give it the sensations of being alive. Like Sisyphus, the king of ancient Carthage who was condemned in Hades to a life of endlessly pushing a giant rock up a hill, only to have it roll back down again, the false self must create and recreate its life over and over and over again. It is desperately afraid of not having the next thing to do, even if it's only to suffer over not yet having the next thing to do. Since this false nature can't really "be" anything in reality, it must endlessly inwardly and outwardly "do" things in order to provide it with the *sensations* of being.

The false self's never-ending dilemma is that all its self-generated sensations are in time. What this means is that sooner or later these self-stimulating sensations, whether pleasurable or painful, are going to come to an end. This is a universal law. All sensations must fade, because sensations are merely echoes of a sort, separate and apart from their cause. Echoes, wherever they temporarily exist, are a kind of phantom. They have an appearance but no real substance. An echo is a shadow. It only *seems* to be there.

Discontentment is a kind of psychic echo. In fact, whatever the unhappiness may be, it is only an inner-echo that is "sounding" within us. As difficult as it may be to understand this at the present time, suffering only *seems* real. It has no *real* life. How is this possible? Here's how. Our inner strains and pains may feel real but then so does a nightmare. But where is the terror once we wake up? It doesn't exist anymore because it was only real as long as we were participating in the bad dream. Try and see this important idea. A painful event, whether it's twenty-four hours or twenty-four years old, echoes within us as a memory of some kind. The emotional "sound" of it when it is recalled makes us feel uncomfortable and discontented. So we set out to isolate this disturbance, identify and resolve it, in order to regain the contentment we say we will feel once this ache goes away.

All of this sounds reasonable, right? Wrong! The catch here, and where we always take the wrong turn, is that the "you" who sets out to turn the discontentment into contentment isn't really you at all! Let's try and understand this amazing new idea by imagining a man lost in a series of deep and dark caverns. He anxiously shouts out "Hello!" and then strains to listen for a response. A heartbeat passes and in the distance he hears "Hello, hello." His spirits surge and off he races in the direction of the caller. He doesn't understand it is only an echo. He doesn't know he is following the sound of his own voice — a voice that is taking him deeper and deeper into the caves and further away from any real help that could deliver him back into the sunlight.

In an illustration like this it is easy for us to see that the man lost in the cave didn't know he was listening to himself. If he had known differently he wouldn't have trusted or followed the sound of his own voice echoing back at him. His mistake was assuming that the voice he was hearing belonged to someone else who wasn't lost like he was.

When it comes to discontentment or any other unhappiness, we are making a similar painful mistake that is taking us further and further away from real rescue. Like the man lost in the caves, we are living with and acting from an equally false assumption. We believe that the inner voices within us, that so readily point out the discontentment in our lives, are doing this pointing from some safe harbor of contentment that we can reach only by following their directions. These persistent and often highly pitched thoughts and feelings project a future well-being for us, a safe harbor — but a harbor that wouldn't be necessary if these same thoughts and feelings hadn't whipped up a storm in the first place! See this! The false self is trying endlessly to get your attention in order to point out to you that there is something missing in your life. Who needs a friend who wakes you up every night to ask if you are asleep?

You are not who you think you are. Your present level of thinking *is* your discontentment because, for the present, the one doing your thinking is Mr. Discontented himself, the false self. I want to make this very clear. *You* are not discontented. *You* have never been unhappy, not now or ever before. No self-described condition of what you have or don't have is at the root of your aching. Your feelings of discontentment and unhappiness, all of these hollow echoes, are the very nature of the false self with which you have unknowingly identified.

Try to remember that what you really want isn't just to *feel* different. No, you want to *be* different. Where feelings invariably fail, Being always triumphs. Who you really are is not separate from the Cause. We can use other words to name this Absolute Source. But again, I say that what we call it is not of any importance. What is important to remember is when something from within you starts telling you that you are all alone, you are not hearing *your* nature but the voice of separateness itself. This is why you must never do anything about your discontentment because *it is not your discontentment*.

Don't be afraid of not having something to do. If you will permit the inner-echoing to fade, it will disappear — and with it, the false self. Choose Being over doing and one day there will be no more pain in what you do or don't do, because you won't be doing anything anymore to prove to yourself that you *are* real. You are and you will know it.

A Secret Strength Greater Than Any Sorrow

Where the author lives, in the scenic Western country, there is abundant wildlife all around his home. There are deer, rabbits, squirrels, coyotes and countless birds of all shapes, colors and sizes. The birds here are especially fortunate because in California's mild climate insects and seed never become really scarce. It's a great life for the birds and their endless singing shows it.

Then there is the cat. She doesn't belong to anyone. The fields around my home were her territory long before I moved in. She'll probably be here when I move out. Her years of independence have honed her hunting skills to a fine edge. Yet her success isn't totally based upon her superior speed or strength. This cat prevails in many instances because she possesses an instinctual intelligence that surpasses that of her prey. The reason the author brings this wildlife story to your attention is he has observed that one of the ways in which this cat hunts can teach us a very important lesson about ourselves and why we keep repeating our painful mistakes. Here is the observation: A cat understands that birds forget. Now let's learn the lesson.

This wild tabby that hunts outside my home knows where the birds gather to feed. Each day she creeps into this small area and, even if she disturbs the birds, she just keeps creeping along. Then, at some designated spot, known only to her, she comes to a dead stop where, for all intents and purposes, she becomes just about invisible. Several minutes later, the birds return and merrily go about their business, even though the cat is still there. She doesn't move a muscle but underneath her weathered coat this cat is so tightly coiled that when at last she springs, it is usually faster than the speed of flight.

In nature this is just the way it is. A bird can only react to what it sees and it generally only sees what is moving. What it can't see, it more or less "forgets." In the animal kingdom this can be a fatal mistake. For us, looking out from the safety of our living rooms at this unyielding world of predator and prey, it is obvious that just because the predator isn't moving doesn't mean it isn't there. Yet what about our inner-world where we find ourselves caught and struggling in the grip of a fear or crisis? We have already learned that whatever negativity is holding us fast cannot and must not be blamed on anyone or anything outside of ourselves. Again, the inner determines the outer.

The question we should be asking ourselves is: How do we reveal these invisible inner-predators that so obviously stalk our psychic system? All of us know what it's like to be jumped on by raging self-doubt or worry, not to mention the host of other dark thoughts and feelings. Let the following questions and answers shed some welcome light on our search for better self-understanding and ultimate self-safety.

Question: I'm beginning to see with the help of these new ideas that what I've suspected all along is true. I have been wasting my time with all of my worldly getaway plans. I need an escape route that leads me away from myself. Any suggestions?
Answer: This may surprise you, but in order to escape yourself you must first stop trying to forget your worries, doubts and fears.

Question: But I thought you said we should try to leave our pains behind us?
Answer: What we said is that you must learn to *understand* them. This new understanding is the only force that can release you from these self-snares because it is your lack of understanding that builds, arms and springs these traps in the first place.

Question: This is so different from what I was always taught. What about the old saying, "Out of sight, out of mind?"
Answer: At the physical level, this idea may hold true but spiritually speaking, in the inner-worlds, nothing could be further from the truth. The great mystic Meister Eckhart understood this. He compassionately warned his students about the dangers of pretenses and self-deception when he told them, "A stone beneath the surface of the ground is just as heavy as a visible one."

Question: I know that what you are saying makes sense, but to tell you the truth, I want to forget my weaknesses. What's wrong with that?
Answer: Trying to forget a fear is like trying to hold an inflated basketball under the water. It takes all of your strength and attention, and in time it must pop to the surface.

Nothing keeps us more aware of a problem than our struggle to forget it. Listen to what Truth is trying to tell you about your strengths instead of listening to your weakness tell you where to hide. The most powerful force in the world for real self-rescue is your own awakened state. Mechanical and unconscious self-defeating behaviors are no match for this higher self-awareness because its strength comes from inner light. Light *always* cancels darkness. Only what is wrong with you wants you to forget what is wrong with you. What is right with you knows that the only thing that is wrong with you is that you don't *know* what is wrong — and that is why you stay pained.

Whenever we bury an unhappiness, we also put out of sight the cause of it. Each crisis is trying to teach us that there is a lesson within it if only we will stay in the classroom. Here is a glimpse of the freedom that awaits you if you will dare to remember yourself when everything in you wants to forget and run away.

By consciously staying with the awareness of your unhappiness, whatever it may be, you will discover one day to your grateful amazement that the pains and aches of this life aren't in *you*. That is correct. All of our unhappiness lies hidden *in our ideas* about who we are and how life should treat us.

The lesson of any painful emotional collision isn't in the crash itself, even though this is what we want to believe. With this convenient answer all we have to do, psychologically speaking, is blame the other driver, get a new car, and drive a different road. This kind of thinking only keeps us crashing with life. What each collision is trying to teach us is that the only thing wrong in our life is our current driver who says he knows the way home when he obviously does not.

How to Change the Life You're Giving Yourself

We meet life, with all of its complex relationships, through what we know. Each daily event, with its dozens of unsuspected twists and turns, challenges us to come up with our best answers. Once our most suitable answer is at hand, we launch it and ourselves into action and watch to see what happens. With each situation this challenge and response process is repeated over and over again, until the condition resolves itself for us, either favorably or not.

The point being made here is that at any given moment we always do what we know. This may seem very obvious, but with closer examination, especially in light of the fact we wish to elevate ourselves and what we are getting from this life, we will discover something very astounding. Read the next three sentences very carefully. I have separated this trio of important ideas for ease of reading, but they are very much connected to each other. Each higher idea leads to the next one, and when they are absorbed all together, they will tell you a great secret.

Before you can get *anything different from this life, you must first* do *something different.*

Before you can do *anything different with your life, you must first* know *something different.*

Before you can know *anything different, you must first suspect and then confirm that it is your present level of understanding that has brought you what you now wish you could change.*

Now let's reverse the order of these right ideas so that we can see how they work from the other way around.

Until you know *something different you cannot* do

anything different.

Until you do *something different you will not* get *anything different.*

And until you really *get something different from your life you cannot know what you have missed and how much more there is to understand.*

Here's the point. Trying to change what you get from life without first changing what you *know* about life is like putting on dry clothes over wet ones and then wondering why you keep shivering. You must stop trying to change what you are getting for yourself and go to work on changing what you are *giving to* yourself.

It is vital for you to realize that life has not held back its riches from you. The truth be known, which it will be, you have been held back from real life by a false nature which thinks life is meant to be suffered through and that all there is to insulate it from a harsh world is what it can win and possess for itself. While there is no denying our world is becoming more and more cruel, there is also no denying that we are the world. Neither our individual world nor the global one can change until the connection between *what we experience* and *who we are* is no longer denied. This is why we must have a new knowledge. Spiritual knowledge isn't something mysterious or out of this world. In fact, spiritual understanding is the most important and practical knowledge a person can possess. It is ultimately what we know about ourselves, about who we really are, that determines the quality of our life.

The truth is we cannot separate our answers from our actions and our actions from their results. They may appear to be individual in their operation because they often occur at different times, but they are really one thing. Intellectually we already know this important concept, but its deep significance hasn't yet become clear. We touched on this earlier. Let's look once more at the old adage, "As ye sow, so shall ye reap." Here again we can see yet a new significance in this New Testament teaching. What you sow is seed or, in this metaphor, your knowledge. What you reap is the crop, or your results. This spiritual knowledge shows us the great importance of reconsidering what we think we know. Life is trying to reach us and teach us, through our experience of it, that we need New and True answers. Any New and True answer is a special kind of intelligent, personal shelter that effortlessly keeps out what is harmful and keeps in what is healthy and life-giving. That is its nature.

Five Exciting New Answers, New Actions and New Results

In order to illustrate how New and True Answers can work for you, the author has gone ahead and written out five examples of these higher answers. You'll see that each New and True Answer also contains a New Action and a New Result. Remember now that each complete section, one through five, is a whole action. In reality, you cannot separate your answers from your actions and your actions from their results. Just as warmth must follow sunlight, so must a higher, happier life follow when Inner-Light is allowed to flourish.

1. **Your New Answer:** Real strength is the refusal to act from weakness.

   Your New Action: See where you have been calling inner-weakness an inner strength; such as calling anxiety concern, or anger righteousness. Dare to live without these false strengths.

   Your New Result: The end of your confusion and pain over why your strength so often fails you. At the same time you will realize the birth of a New and True strength that never turns into its weak opposite.

2. **Your New Answer:** Have the courage to proceed even while knowing that you are afraid.

Your New Action: Dare to take one shaky step after another.

Your New Result: Freedom from a life of fear because fear cannot exist whenever insight is valued above feeling frightened.

3. **Your New Answer:** Forgiveness is the personal understanding that except for circumstance there is no real difference between you and your offender.

Your New Action: In spite of all the inner-screams to the contrary, dare to treat your trespasser as you would want to be treated.

Your New Result: When you stop punishing others for their weakness, you will stop punishing yourself for yours.

4. **Your New Answer:** Compassion is the conscious refusal to add to another person's suffering, even though it may seem to increase yours.

Your New Action: Dare to shoulder one hundred times the mental and emotional weight you think you can carry.

Your New Result: Contained right within the suffering is the glimpse that there is no sufferer.

5. **Your New Answer:** Real hope is the fact that there is always a Higher Solution.

Your New Action: See that any time you feel pained or defeated, it is only because you insist on clinging to what doesn't work. Dare to let go and you won't lose a thing except for a punishing idea.

Your New Result: A new life that fears no inner or outer challenge since defeat can only exist in the absence of a willingness to learn.

Now that you have studied these five New and True Answers, you may wish to write down some of your own. This is highly profitable for accelerating your inner growth. Don't be discouraged if at first you can't come up with any new ideas. There is great gain in your efforts because even the smallest attempt to find new answers *is* a new answer! The more you work with truthful principles, the more they will work for you. Always remember when you work with powerful Higher Ideas such as these that there are many temporarily unknown parts of yourself that may try to mislead you. They know that your growing true spiritual insight will lead you away from their harmful influence and deliver you to True Safety. No matter what the harmful voices within may say, whosoever puts the Truth first will never lose anything except for that which was *never* real in the first place.

The Secret of Permanent Pleasure

There is a higher pleasure which makes all other pleasures seem like pebbles next to pearls; but to claim this rich treasure for your own you must dare to sail where others claim there is nothing but an edge that drops off into nothing.

As with the undertaking of any important expedition, we must be properly prepared, so we need to spend a few moments laying down the necessary groundwork for our inner- journey. This new knowledge, coupled with your wish to succeed in your quest, will carry you forward and out of your old limited life and into this brand new world of higher pleasure. It just isn't physically possible to convey to you the importance of these new ideas. The author has done everything in his power to make this material come alive for you, the reader. However, nothing brings higher ideas to life more strongly than your sincere wish to understand them. If you will do this part, your part, the Truth will do the rest for you. The author can point to a meadow brimming with blossoms, but you must do the walking if you ever wish to stand among all the colorful flowers.

Let's imagine for a moment that you are feeling chilled. You tell someone how cold you are and, to your surprise, they respond by giving you a picture postcard of a roaring fireplace. You are certainly stunned, but definitely not any warmer. Why? Because the picture of the flames, the *idea* of a fire is not the warmth itself. Again, the idea of a glass of water is not the water itself, and an idea cannot quench your thirst anymore than the words "life raft" will float you if you cling to them in a storm.

All of this may seem so obvious to you that you wonder where the author is headed. Here is our destination. In our prior illustrations with simple objects, we understand that *the thought is not the thing*. But this important insight suddenly seems to break down when it comes to our own thoughts and feelings about ourselves. We believe that these movements within us are indeed what they call themselves.

For instance, who hasn't felt sad and then had the thought, "I am sad?" There very well may be a genuine feeling of sadness; but in *reality* there is no one there who is sad.

Just as we agreed earlier that the thought is never the thing, so this same Higher Principle holds true when it comes to your feelings. This next sentence will help you to understand what we have been saying. Read it several times so that its meaning will reach home. Sadness or gladness is *something you feel, not something you are.*

A feeling is just that — a feeling. It has no true independent existence. When a feeling is pleasurable you want it to go on, because you have mistakenly identified with its pleasant sensations. You think you *are* that feeling. This misplaced sense of self wouldn't present any problems, except that as your pleasurable feelings fade, which all feelings must do, so does the you that was feeling pleased. Now all you can do is feel displeased and so you start the pleasure-seeking cycle all over again.

"This explains why I sometimes feel trapped by my own schemes to make myself feel good. It's like being on an amusement ride that won't let you get off because it never really ends. How can I break out of this circle of pleasure and pain?"

"Ponder deeply this next Higher Idea. It will help you to start going up instead of around. *You think that what you are looking for is pleasure, but what you are really seeking is permanence.*"

"What a fascinating idea, but isn't permanence just a feeling, too?"

"No. There is the pleasure of permanence which is not a feeling but a level of being. This elevated state of awareness may include all of the various feelings as they come and go, pleasant or not, but it remains effortlessly undisturbed and undiminished by either emotional ebb or swell. Your pleasure is that *you are* — not what you feel."

"What do I have to do to reach this elevated condition?"

"You will be well on your way when your wish to remain aware of your pleasures is as strong as your wish to lose yourself in their feelings."

"Can you explain to me why this kind of special awareness is so important?"

"Certainly. Only the awareness of your pleasures allows you to enjoy them without feeling as though you are disappearing when they do."

"That makes perfect sense. How does it work?"

"Before I give you an answer, you must understand the importance of finding out how it works for yourself. This is the only way you can ever really be certain that Personal Permanence is possible. This new awareness is like the powerful lighthouse that stands both within and apart from all of the tempests that may rage around it. Its bright beam remains effortlessly steady even as it shines out and on through all kinds of stormy weather. Nothing disturbs or alters its essence because light has a totally different nature from any other force it may encounter out at sea. Similarly, your True Nature cannot be carried away whether your emotional seas blow furious or present a picture-perfect horizon. You remain pleased because now your real pleasure is in your awareness that *you* are what is constant."

The author highly recommends that you go back and review the section in chapter three entitled, "Higher Awareness Through Self-Observation." It will give you additional insights into this new kind of awareness that leads to permanent higher pleasure.

Here are five points to ponder to help you obtain a new kind of permanent pleasure.

1. *If your pleasures begin as feelings, they will end that way . . . only the feelings of fading pleasure are not always that pleasant.*

2. *The false self is only as content as its last thought about itself, while your True Nature is content within itself.*

3. *The pursuit of a pleasure to ease a pain is like running after a breeze to cool you down.*

4. *Trying to find pleasure in your feelings alone is like looking for a staircase on a rainbow.*

5. *You are not supposed to win over this world; you are intended to raise yourself above it.*

CHAPTER 5

Letting Go Into the Power Flow

In the early 1900's, before the age of super highways, supermarkets, and the giant food manufacturers, small farmers used to truck or cart each season's harvest to a centralized buyers' market that had been set up for their particular region. Some farmers, more isolated than others, might have had to travel hundreds of miles just to sell their crops. For these hardy people who lived and worked the small, outlying farms, this was about the only time they would see any other people outside of their own families. Everyone looked forward to going to these great open markets. There were crafts to exchange and store-bought goods to buy, the newest catalogs to see and the warmth of at least a thousand hellos. All of this, plus the hard-earned financial rewards that come with the close of another season, always made marketing their harvest an exciting, happy time for everyone involved.

That's why, as he stood there taking the whole festival feeling in, the old farmer couldn't understand why anyone should be standing around looking tired and distressed. But sure enough, leaning up against the side of one of the large tented areas stood a very unhappy young farmer.

"What could possibly be this boy's problem?" the old man wondered to himself. The recent weather had been more than kind and every farmer at the market, including this young man, had brought in a bumper crop. He thought about it for a moment and decided to do the neighborly thing. He walked over to the young man.

"Anything I can help you with?" he asked, as gently as he knew how. When he got no response, he tried another approach: "Hope you don't mind me asking. It's just that you look like maybe you could use a helping hand."

The young farmer looked up at his elder without raising his head. "Thanks, but there's nothing you can do to help."

"How do you know?" the old man asked back.

A long moment passed, then the young farmer spoke, "You don't understand," he said. "It's that dumb tractor of mine. Sometimes it's more trouble than it's worth."

"What's wrong with it?"

"I don't really know. It's harder to use some days than others. The dumb thing just tuckers me out sometimes to where me and my family don't want to farm anymore."

Something wasn't adding up in the mind of the old farmer as he listened to the young man speak. "Harder to use, you say? Maybe I could take a look at it sometime. I'm pretty fair with these new contraptions."

"Sure," the young man's eyes brightened momentarily, "but I don't think there's much you can do. We'd be pleased to have you come by anyway, and we'll fix you a nice supper for your trouble."

So they exchanged directions.

A few short weeks later, after half a day's travel, the old farmer rolled his horse-drawn, tool-laden cart onto the young man's farmland. Straight ahead of him in a distant field he could see the young farmer and his wife, along with their two sons.

They were struggling to push a small tractor along the raised crop beds.

"Hello!" the old man cried out as his cart drew into hearing range. "She's still not running right, I see."

The young farmer smiled back at him and said, "What do you mean? It's going good today!"

The old farmer sat there shocked for a moment. It just couldn't be. He knew he had to ask the next question, but he had a hard time getting the words out.

"Do you mean to tell me," the old man tried to find the right pitch, "that you always push this tractor to make it work?"

The young man looked back at him as though a little irritated with such a stupid question. "Well, how else do you get it to do what you want?"

Realizing everything all at once about the young man's deep weariness and defeated appearance earlier on at the farmers' market, the old farmer said as calmly as he knew how, "My son, a tractor is something you are meant to ride on, not push!"

It took quite a bit of explaining, several trips to town, and a lot of greasy work, but by the time the old man finally said farewell to the young man and his family, the small tractor was up and running in high gear. And so was everyone's spirit. At last everything was as it was intended to be. Life was good.

The author realizes, as he is sure you do, that such a story probably never did or ever could happen. However, this tale of the misunderstood tractor contains a highly valuable lesson for anyone who is genuinely tired of pushing against life. Stress exists because you insist! It's really that simple. It is your mistaken belief that you must push life in the direction you choose that keeps you in a strained and unhappy relationship with it. Your wish to have power over life comes from this wrong relationship with life. Reality has its own effortless course, and you can either embrace its way or struggle endlessly with yours. *You do not need power to flow*. Why push when you can learn to ride?

With a new kind of effort you can climb aboard an entirely new kind of life that always has fair skies and the wind at its back. In his amazing book, *The Power of Your Supermind,* Vernon Howard talks about the possibility of this special kind of effortless life.

> *"People waste their lives trying to get things done for them, without strained effort on their part. There is such a way, but it comes only after personal effort of the right kind. It is like flying a kite. If you act rightly by holding the kite up to passing winds, it will naturally fly by itself. Now, life itself is our support, which means the need for finding the true life of the Supermind and not living from imitation.*
>
> "Tao Teh King, *the wise book of the East, comments on this. It says that when a man abides in the Way, his satisfactions are inexhaustible.*
>
> *"Suppose a small child wants to fly a kite but knows nothing about natural winds. He sets the kite on the ground and tries to fly it by blowing heavily with his breath. His frustration could make him receptive to an older child's information about the wind. Then, by replacing wrong effort with right, his kite flies effortlessly."* [1]

The Sure Cure for Whatever Disturbs You

Imagine a nicely dressed couple seated at an elegant table in a sophisticated restaurant. They are talking over a matter of great concern to both of them. At the beginning of their conversation he is cordial and relaxed and she is smiling warmly. As the evening progresses and individual intentions are brought to the surface, the man begins to edge up on his seat and his attitude takes on an edge as well. Her once engaging smile draws down into a thin, tense expression. Each of them is now

---

[1] Vernon Howard, *The Power of Your Supermind,* (Prentice Hall, 1967).

steadily sending special signals to the other. These invisible unspoken messages are saying, "Don't push me too far;" and behind these silent messages lurks what both of them know is the real bottom line — "Don't make me use force."

With few exceptions, most everyone will sympathetically agree that the use of force in any given situation should be the last resort. However, this short illustrative drama points out an important and unseen psychological fact about what is really going on just beneath our carefully kept appearances. And that is we *always* revert to some kind of force when things don't go our way. Why else do you think that a person seeks power in this life? No one seeks power to do good unless it's first for the good of himself. This prevailing popular philosophy of self-empowerment is justified by the thought that once I have enough then I can give to others from my abundance. The only problem with this is it's just one lie perpetuating another. First of all, for the false nature there is never enough of anything; and that's beside the fact that you don't need power to do Good. Good is its own power. We seek power because we want the force to make things go the way we want; to crush the small and large rebellions and disturbances wherever they may arise, whether at home or at the work place.

Power, who has it and who doesn't, seems to determine in this world who pushes and who gets shoved. And given our preference, if we must choose one, we would rather be doing the pushing. The only problem is that on the level of this field of choices, whether to push or be pushed, everyone loses because push always comes to shove. The really incredible part of all of this, as we are about to learn from our self-studies, is that there is no *real* worldly or personal power to be found here at all. Even more amazingly, we will discover to our great relief that none is needed. That's right. This is because there is a third choice. This third and higher choice is *the choice to be left alone*. The following paragraph will help you to understand this new and truly powerful idea:

> *There is no power on earth that can make you feel safe and secure, because it isn't this world that threatens or disturbs you. You seek worldly and personal power because* you are dominated by your own thoughts and feelings. *It is your own undeveloped nature that punishes you because it doesn't as yet understand that the disturbance it perceives as being outside of itself is itself. And so this unconscious nature keeps you ever seeking power and authority in the hopes that with enough of it, you will eventually have the force to be able to control your life. This is like throwing a rock into a pond to quiet the ripples. The more you toss in, the more waves you get. That is why what you really want is to leave yourself alone.*

"I think I understand what you are getting at, but if the powers of social and economic forces can't make me feel safe and secure, what will?"

"First, let's briefly review what we have just gone over. We seek self-power because we are dominated by our own feelings. We are taken over by our own reactions. This is painful for us because our original nature, our True Nature, longs to be free and unencumbered by self-limiting, self-defeating, compulsive thoughts and feelings. The problem is at our present undeveloped level, we believe that another person or event is causing our unhappy feelings. We want power over them in the hope that it will give us power over our punishing feelings. Can you see that this approach to self-command is doomed from its ill-conceived beginning?"

"Yes, definitely, only now I'm afraid it seems as though there is no way out. Where do we look for the power we need to be happy?"

"Look for this power not in a person, place, possession, idea or belief, but through the new understanding that your higher, permanent nature needs no power outside of itself in order to be in charge of an inner or outer attacker. Its strength is what the author calls the *Silent Force*. It alone can do for you what you have been unable to do for yourself."

"What is this Silent Force? How do I make it work for me?"

"If you really want to know the answer to your question, nothing on earth can stop you from knowing. Let me tell you a little bit about it. *The Silent Force is the understanding that you need not answer to any disturbance within you.* You must not respond. You have been taught by wrong example and false traditions that negative thoughts and feelings such as fear, anger and hatred are something you are responsible for; that they belong to you. You are indeed responsible *for* them, but not *to* them. Inner aches and dark feelings are not yours. They never have been and they never will be no matter how much these inner-impostors try to convince you otherwise."

"I like what you are saying. Could you explain a little more? What do you mean when you say I am responsible for my fears but not *to* them?"

"Yes, it is unnatural for any human being to be dominated by anything. Your only true responsibility is to understand this higher fact. And your corrected understanding places you in the right relationship with all gloomy thoughts and defeated feelings; which is that you simply have nothing to do with them. We are not saying to act or pretend as though dark feelings don't exist. This is very important to understand because pretending as though a rampaging elephant isn't there or that it's a cute bunny may feel good temporarily but it leaves you in danger. Seeing the elephant and recognizing it for what it is allows Intelligence to take you where you need to be — which is out of the jungle."

No grief or disturbance of any kind is yours. These huge inner-shadows with all their howlings may be present, but where is it written that they belong to you? When we walk through a zoo, we don't identify with the shrieks and whines of the animals, so why do we fall into the self-confining cage of trying to make what is dark into what is light? Ever tried yelling at a bunch of chattering chimps or squawking birds to quiet them down? Insisting that they settle down just disturbs them all the more. Inwardly, the same law holds true. When we seek some power to make a fear go away, all we have done is empower the fear. There is no power that can make light out of darkness. Remember this lesson the next time you feel compelled to help yourself out of a dark inner-thought or feeling. Remember the Silent Force. Go silent! This silence and inner-light will do for you what you have not been able to do for yourself. It will turn the dark inner-skies into pleasant blue ones. Go silent. Let the threatening clouds of thoughts and feelings go by. Behind them is the sun.

Let Go of the Fear of Being No One

Why is it that we will challenge and then work to change the world's opinions as they concern us, but we never question our own beliefs no matter how much personal pressure, stress and anxiety they may produce? For example, we wouldn't dream of diving for sunken treasure in our bathtub because we know that the best we can hope to find there are a few plastic pearls. And yet we still dive headlong into this world every day to try and become Someone. Over and over again we sink ourselves into some new scheme that promises greater self-confirmation in spite of the fact that the best we have ever realized so far is a temporary kind of self-elevation that has never failed to turn into its painful opposite of self-doubt. Here's the point. *It is our belief we must be Someone that punishes us, not the world that won't confirm our beliefs.*

With patient self-study and the help of Truthful ideas we can learn to lead an entirely New Life. I know I have stressed this time and again but it is so important for us to understand. The Truth is not something impractical and hopelessly distant from us. It is as close and immediate as our wish to understand why it is that we keep hurting ourselves and others. With this right intention to guide us, let's look at this wish that we all have to become Someone. And during our investigation let's work to keep in mind it is what we can see about this world that is our Real Safety and not what we can win from it.

Everybody wants to be a Someone. Why? Just ask anyone and they will tell you in so many words: Somebody who is Someone has power. Power is necessary; without it we can't isolate and protect ourselves from a crushing world of others who want at all cost what we want — which is to become Someone. In short, the idea of becoming someone contains the unquestioned and pervasive belief that whatever measure of safety, security and happiness we may win in this life depends directly upon just how much of a Someone we can succeed at becoming. This is, whether spoken or not, how almost everyone on earth believes. And it is this very belief, this treasure hunt in the tub, that holds the seed of sorrow for all of mankind.

Neatly hidden within this false belief, not unlike the too-tempting poison apple offered to Snow White by the evil witch, is this belief's *opposite* — an opposite which lurks and shouts within the psychic system of each unsuspecting believer just outside his ability to see and hear its message — but well within his capacity to feel its presence. And this feeling is fear, because this opposite clearly implies that if we *don't* become Someone we will never know safety and security. Fear's powerful, almost unshakable, silent implication is that if we don't become Someone in our own eyes or in the eyes of others, we will have no power; and being powerless we will perish and vanish. This is what drives men and women to the point of collapse. It is not the promise of being Someone who is ceaselessly pleased but rather the threat of unceasing unhappiness that compels us to succeed no matter what the personal or global cost. Let's put it this way: We have not been running *to* something, that goal or that dream, we have been running *from* something. We have been running from the fear of being no one.

As we will see, this is an unresolvable race because we are tied to whatever we avoid. That's right. So far, fear has set the course and the pace. This explanation sheds some light on why it is so hard for us to relax, even when it is the time for it. The facts are the more we try to become Someone, or even seem to succeed at the task, the more in jeopardy we feel. The good news is that this problem is nothing new nor is it its real solution. Inspired men and women throughout the ages have come to understand these self-defeating inner-traps and, in doing so, have won lasting freedom for themselves. You can do the same.

J. Krishnamurti, a brilliant world philosopher and teacher, spoke of this invisible unhappiness over fifty years ago while lecturing to a gathering of students in Ojai, California. In this talk he also revealed the secret for final self-victory.

> *"If you are poor, mentally, emotionally, physically, you want to be rich, do you not? You want to have a rich mind, strong emotion. Now that is but pursuing an opposite, and the opposite contains the thing from which you are escaping. What you are pursuing holds that from which you are running away. When you are poor, you want to be rich, and you know by contrast what it is to be rich. You are pursuing wealth in your mind, and thus you are creating the opposite through your desire; whereas, in the recognition of the fact that you are poor,* and in trying to be free of the idea of poverty, *you destroy the opposite.*
>
> *"If you dislike someone, it is useless for you to say you must love him; that breeds hypocrisy. But if you try to be free of the idea of dislike, you are becoming free of the idea of distinction — both like and dislike. You cannot do this mentally; you cannot say, " 'I must be free of dislike,' and intellectually deceive yourself. The recognition of the fact of that which you are, without trying to escape from it, leads to freedom from the opposites."* [2]

How to Let Your Worries Roll By

Years ago, the author used to enjoy watching a television program called *Spanky and Our Gang*. Each show featured the heart-warming antics of a group of young children who, in their friendship, had banded together to form a club. Perhaps you remember some of the characters. There was Alfalfa, Spanky, Froggy, Darla, Buckwheat and many others. One show I want to tell you about always remains in my mind. You'll see why in a minute. Here's a brief summary.

The boys were going to be in big trouble because the teacher had told them that the next day she was going to give them a surprise test. So on that moonless evening, late into the night, they broke into their own classroom to steal the test to learn its answers. Right in the middle of the whole caper, one of the kids, a black boy named Buckwheat, got tangled up in some rope and started causing a racket. In the ensuing noise and growing confusion everyone decided to make a break for it. Kids were running everywhere. All Buckwheat knew was that he too wanted out of this scary situation. Unfortunately, and as yet unknown to him, he still trailed the rope, which had gotten twisted around his ankle. As luck would have it, the loose end of this rope then got wrapped around the wheeled base of the classroom's science skeleton. The next thing poor Buckwheat knew was that a terrible creature was chasing him and that, try as he might, he couldn't outrun its clattering shape.

This was hilarious for everyone but poor Buckwheat. The faster he ran, so did his worst nightmare. He couldn't shake the trailing skeleton because he was tied to it! Do you see the connection? If Buckwheat could have somehow understood his situation, all he would have had to do was stop running. The frightening apparition that was chasing him would have just

---

[2] J. Krishnamurti, *Early Writings,* (Chetana, 1971).

rolled right by him and then, coming to the end of its tether, it would have toppled over. Its only power was that which Buckwheat gave to it in his fear. And Buckwheat was only afraid because he didn't understand.

You can understand. You can cut yourself loose from all of your fears and worries. There is no question that this new kind of self-work will take a special effort on your part. But you are not alone. The Truth wants you to succeed. Once you understand that nothing real is threatening you, where is your need to anxiously protect yourself? Once you know, which you will, that you have already been given an independent, timeless identity, you need never worry again about making yourself into Someone. This is real success.

Never Feel Trapped By Life Again

Roy knew he was in big trouble. His little hand that had slipped so easily into the cookie jar was stuck there. He couldn't get his hand out. It was like a nightmare. His mother had clearly told him "no sweets before dinner" just before she left to pick up his older brother at school. Now they were back and walking in the front door. In a second she would be inside. Too late to think it through, little Roy ran up to his mother waving his hand in the jar. "Mom! Help me! I was in the kitchen minding my own business when all of a sudden the cookie jar jumped up and tried to swallow my hand!"

Times have changed, but not our struggles. We still get our hands caught and we are still blaming the various cookie jars. Only now the things that trap us cause us much more pain than did the innocent events of our youth. The truth is we haven't learned much in spite of our years of tears. Blaming a trap that you walked into is like getting angry at a French fry that was too hot to put in your mouth. The only power that any trap in life holds over us is our own lack of understanding that draws us into its snare in the first place. In the highest sense, and perhaps most poetically, we always trap ourselves. Nowhere is this more true than when it comes to what I call the *Power Trap*.

As with all inner invisible snares, the power trap looks like a promise but holds only a punishment. The *only* way out of this or any other inner-trap is to become wiser than the master trap maker — better known as the false self. This rogue lower nature has many tricks up its dark sleeve designed just to keep us struggling in its grasp. One of its most clever deceits is to make us believe that the unhappy experience of *feeling* trapped is the trap itself. The false self knows that if it can convince us to struggle with trying to change the experience that the *real* trap, the *cause* of the suffering, will go on undetected. The truth is we are *never* trapped by any experience. The painful experience of *feeling* trapped is the effect of the trap, *not the trap itself.* The more we try to change the experience, the more we unknowingly tighten the jaws of the real inner invisible trap.

This is why wise men of all ages have placed so much emphasis on the importance of self-awareness which we call Seeing. The only strength any psychological snare may possess is in *our* unawareness of its presence. Choose inner-lighting over experience-fighting and we dissolve the trap. Once the trap disappears, where is the pain or the need to struggle and escape? Let me tell you a true personal story to illustrate this extremely important idea. By necessity, I will change the characters as well as the location of the story, but a truer tale has not been told. See if it doesn't reveal to you what your heart already knows.

The Best Kept Secret in the World

Sitting there at the softly lit outdoor bar, surrounded by powerful and elegant people, Alexis felt this was the night she had been waiting for all her life. As the newest junior partner in the firm, she had been, at last, invited up to the chief executive officer's palatial estate for his semi-annual big bash. Corporate giants from all over the world made it a point to attend these parties and only the "who's who" received invitations. She had heard that here was where the real deals were put together.

These men and women were the power brokers and she wanted to be a part of it all.

But unknown to Alexis that evening was going to be powerful for her in a way she could have never guessed. Even today she can still vividly recall the events that so profoundly changed her life. It all started when she walked over to the vice-president of her division and struck up a relaxed but probing conversation. After all, she was the bright and upcoming new executive, so it seemed natural to question him about what her future held in store. Besides, everyone knew that he was powerful in his own right and just to be seen talking with him meant you were someone of some significance. The next thirty minutes were almost like heaven. Her executive officer told her, in so many words, that she would go on to become a major force in the industry — a power in her own right.

As their conversation was coming to a close, Alexis noticed that her boss had suddenly become visibly distracted. This made her feel somewhat anxious. What if she had bored him? However, much to her relief, a beat later she saw that the reason he was acting so strangely was that his boss, the chief executive officer himself, had just entered the room and was motioning over to them. A moment later she watched on in silence as the two most important people in her life walked over to a corner of the room and started talking. She tried to imagine what important business they were discussing. Maybe she was the topic of conversation. Wouldn't that be exciting?

Against her better judgement, but well in line with her insatiable curiosity, Alexis found an out-of-the-way place next to them that was out of their sight but within earshot of their dialogue. What she overheard during the next few minutes broke against her like an ocean wave rolling up to a sand castle. It felt like a whole portion of her life had fallen into the surge and had been washed away. Somehow it just didn't add up. She was more troubled by her own reaction to their conversation than she was by the content of what she had just overheard. After all, all that had transpired was that her boss had just spent the last few minutes quietly but anxiously asking his boss the exact same questions about his future that she had been asking him less than ten minutes before. What in the world was going on? She wanted all the cards on the table, even if it meant finding out she had been hiding some from herself. She wanted to know and nothing was going to stop her.

So, from that moment on, Alexis secretly shadowed her boss's boss around the party. This man was the chief executive officer of their company and she wanted to see just who he talked to and what he talked about. Near the end of the evening she thought she had lost sight of him until she realized that he was standing out on the edge of the patio talking with another gentleman. It only took a second for her to recognize this partner in conversation as the chairman of the board of the eighth-largest corporation in America.

Neither of them saw her ease over to the sliding glass doors and no one dancing by her at the party realized what she was doing. But she knew. And if she hadn't already prepared herself for what she was about to overhear, Alexis probably would have collapsed on the spot. However, in the back of her mind, she had long suspected what was now being played out before her.

As she strained to listen in on their muffled conversation, she heard her boss's boss asking this powerful chairman what he thought the future held in store for him! Alexis knew in that very moment that she had stumbled on to one of the best kept secrets in the world. That thirty seconds of dialogue between those two men explained everything to her. Here was the root of her longstanding and deep-seated insecurity. She now understood her doubts about solemn promises made and never kept by others. No wonder everybody, including the so-called power brokers of this world, trembles before unexpected events. In a flash, Alexis understood all of this and more. Her eyes had been opened. Her personal pursuit of power had so blinded her that until that moment she had never allowed herself to consider what was now so painfully obvious.

She had been an unwitting, unconscious player in a global game of make-believe, in which each of the players involved pretends to have enough power to help someone else less powerful secure their future. However, each of these so-called power players doesn't have quite enough power to put their *own* fears and doubts to rest. And so, they are in turn compelled to look to yet another player who they can only hope will somehow help them.

Everyone is so busy looking for something or someone else to give them this power that no one sees that no one has it! Why couldn't she see this before? She had been giving her life away day after day, struggling to climb a power ladder that was powerless to lift her. She had been trapped playing in a game where the only prize was the hope of winning. From the so-called bottom rung of this power ladder all the way to its so-called top, everyone on it is in the exact same position. All are afraid. She had been afraid to see it but now she *knew* it. That's why it's a game of make-believe. Those who play have shut their eyes to the fact that depending on someone to help them who can't really help themselves is a recipe for fear, anxiety and resentment. It's like two men who are lost and wandering in the desert with no water. When by chance they meet, each of them pretends to have water so that the other will share his. Both go thirsty. No matter how many people may agree to sit down to an imaginary feast, all will walk away hungry.

Up until that evening, Alexis thought she wanted power over others. Now she knew that all she'd ever wanted was to be in charge of herself. All along she had been so certain she had to win the approval and support of others. Now she knew the only important victory was for her to win true independence.

Let's summarize some of the important points in this chapter section.

1. *We fall into the Power Trap any time we go looking for a strength outside of ourself instead of revealing to ourself the inner-weakness that sent us seeking.*

2. *Looking for a new strength to solve an old weakness is a waste of time and only makes us weaker. What is needed is New Understanding.*

3. *Real power* never *seeks power. You need no power outside the strength of your own Awakened Original Nature.*

4. *If you are seeking power you are under the power of that which has no power and, regardless of appearances, you will become increasingly powerless.*

5. *You can only have the power to possess the parts of yourself that you are willing to see you have given away.*

6. *Trying to arrive at true independence by depending on others is like trying to reach the stars by climbing into a hole.*

7. *No man is powerful as long as power is his need.*

8. *The power of the Truth is that only in its Light can we see where we have been calling a weakness a strength. Real strength appears all by itself once we stop acting from weakness.*

Don't Miss This Life-Changing Moment

Even though the Truth is never further away from us than our wish for its awakening and self-healing insight, there are distinct moments in life when it comes closer to us. Unfortunately, almost all of these important, potentially life-changing moments are entirely missed because what is wrong with us, our false nature, always sees Truth as an attacking enemy. Let me show you what I mean so that the next time Truth makes an unexpected appearance in your life you will recognize it for what it is — a friendly and beneficial force that is on *your* side. Permitting the Truth to do what it is intended to do will permit you to be what you want to be — which is happy.

Never are the healing powers of the Truth so close by as when a crisis is at hand. A crisis always precedes any real inner-advancement because real spiritual growth is a process of *removing* self-blocking thoughts and feelings. The reason a crisis must precede each new level of authentic self-unity is that the crisis, whatever it may be, points out where we have been holding onto a particular belief, a shaky pretense, or some flattering but deceptive self-image that is in conflict with reality. Where there is conflict there is always pain; and by the time this unconscious kind of psychological or emotional pain reaches the level of our consciousness, we generally experience it as some kind of a crisis. This explains why *a crisis is a close encounter of the Truthful kind.* The previously invisible internal conflict, which is always at the root of any personal crisis, is now temporarily visible. We can say this in another way. A crisis arises when some inner-lie we have unconsciously been telling ourselves is about to surface and be seen as a lie. Let's take an example or two.

Maybe a man pictures himself as always being in control of his own life, but now he's suddenly aware that he can't stop drinking — or talking — or endlessly worrying. He has reached a turning point.

A woman has always thought of herself as being loving and kind, but all at once she begins to notice how critical and cruel her thoughts are towards others. She sees that she only does things for others to have them think of her as being kind, and this fills her day with resentments. She has reached a turning point.

In both instances, where the terrible cost of living from lying but flattering self-images has suddenly become conscious, the only alternative that the false self has, as the author of these self-deceptive lies, is to start blaming everyone and everything for the unhappy circumstances. This system of self-subterfuge is almost fail-safe for the false self. By seeing to it that everything outside of it is constantly laid to blame, it keeps you fighting with life instead of learning from it. It is really very cunning. The more you take the side of defending what is wrong in you, the more the Truth that exposed the unconscious wrongness appears to be against you. Try and see this. It would be extra good inner-work for you to try to connect this important insight with what we have just learned about inner-traps.

The Truth never causes pain. The only pain in a crisis is the false self's resistance to the Truth. *A crisis only becomes a breaking point when we fail to use it as a turning point.* In order to transform a crisis into a personal turning point in your life, you must wish to be shown the lesson *in* the crisis rather than allow yourself to be convinced *by* it that the world is against you. This Higher Wish, followed by your willingness to endure a new kind of pain, gives birth to a Higher Consciousness in you that belongs to your True Nature. This Elevated Consciousness never has to solve a crisis because it never has one in the first place.

"I was with you all the way until you got to the 'new kind of pain' part. I want to be free of the pain, not have a new kind to worry about!"

"This new kind of pain is the temporary pain of consciously enduring what is necessary to end your pain. We can talk about it in two ways — both are the same. This new pain is your bold refusal to let whatever conflict you are experiencing go back under ground . . . or . . . It is your agreement to keep this inner-conflict conscious or visible long enough so that you can see its cause."

"What does that accomplish? Why not just forget it and go

play, or just wait until the pain fades?"

"We've all tried similar approaches. Pretending that the pain has gone away only compounds its punishment when it returns — which it always does if its cause has not been eliminated. Temporary relief is just that, especially when it comes to inner-conflict. This sometimes inner-silence is like the tense quiet between rounds of shelling on the battlefield. There is no real rest for anyone waiting there. On the other hand, let's look at the benefits of what happens when we keep the conflict conscious. Let's take an example. Suppose that the cause of a man's conflict is his pretense to be wise and strong. He wants others to think of him as a source of strength and stability — someone to be depended upon in times of a crisis. Of course, part of the reason he wants others to see him in this way is so that he can feel it's true about himself. And yet, for all of his endless advice to others on how to soar above their problems, he knows that he can't lift himself even an inch off the ground when his own needs are the greatest. He is in a crisis condition. He can either choose to continue pretending he has a strength he doesn't — which is to avoid the crisis — or he can enter the crisis, where his heightened awareness of his pretense will not only destroy the pretense but also all of the fear and self-doubt that must accompany it."

"How can just the awareness of my pretense destroy it?"

"Because no one needs to suffer! Before the light of this new and Higher Awareness made everything clear to you, the false self had you convinced that you needed to keep pretending in order to feel good about yourself! *The pain in this pretense was making you anxious — not happy.* You only thought you needed to pretend to be good or kind, wise or strong. What you really needed was to see through your need to pretend. Your True Nature is all you need. Let it show you what you don't need."

In his book, *The Mystic Path to Cosmic Power,* Vernon Howard uses the following dialogue to illustrate how this new

Awareness can clear away our fears and confusion:

> " *'I don't understand. You say that awareness of anxiety dissolves it. I know how anxious I am and still it persists.'*
>
> " *'Feeling anxiety is not the same as awareness. When you merely feel anxious, you are identified with it; you are so close you can't see it. If you close your eyes and feel a round object with your fingers, you may worry that it is a bomb. Open your eyes and you see it is a harmless ball. Likewise, as we awaken to see things as they really are, our pains disappear.'* "[3]

The Secret of Having Everything You Want

Everyone wonders whether or not there is one Great Secret for truly successful living. There is. And it is not a secret. It has been quietly, steadily telling itself right in front of us all along. We just couldn't hear it over the clatter and chatter of our own secret demands. Listen quietly for a moment. Everything can change right now. Learning to hear this Supreme Secret is no more difficult than choosing whether to swim against a current or to let it carry you safely to the shore. Let it speak its wisdom to that secret part of you that can not only hear what it is saying but that is, in reality, its very voice. Listen to it now. It is saying, "*Want What Life Wants.*" Think about it. Locked within these four simple words is the secret of an uncompromising power for effortless living; a new kind of power that never fails to place you on the winning side of any situation. Why? Because when you *want what Life wants*, your wish is for *Life* itself.

"What if I don't like what life brings to me?"

"Try to see that it is not what life has brought to you that you don't like. It is your reactions that turn the gift of life into

---

[3]Vernon Howard, *The Mystic Path to Cosmic Power*, (Prentice Hall, 1967).

the resentment of it."

"I don't want to sound ungrateful, but speaking plainly, I'm tired of being unhappy. What difference does it make why I feel this way?"

"Because these unhappy feelings are born out of life failing to conform to your ideas of what you need to be happy. This shows you, if you will see it, that Life itself isn't denying you happiness. It is your ideas about life that have failed you. Give up these wrong ideas instead of giving up on life. Be increasingly willing to see they are nothing but a constant source of conflict. Your false nature will tell you that you must have these self-protecting ideas; that you can't live without them or you will lose something valuable. What you must do, in spite of any such protest to the contrary, is to see that you can't live with them. All you will lose is your unhappiness."

Here are two lists that will not only make these life-healing ideas more personal for you, but they will help you to help yourself make a higher choice when it comes to what you really want from life. It would be valuable to study and then compare the lists to each other. You may wish to add to either list some of your own insights, which I highly encourage you to do.

Let's look at what happens *When You Want What You Want:*

1. *You are often nervous and anxious because life may not cooperate with your plans.*

2. *You are willing to sacrifice whatever it takes to get what you want, and this may include your integrity.*

3. *You are usually scheming in some way to win your next victory.*

4. *You are either in a battle or recovering from one.*

5. *You are unable to rest quietly when you need to.*

6. *You are easily angered when someone or something gets in your way.*

7. *You are forever driven to want something else.*

8. *You are against anyone else who also wants what you want.*

9. *You are certain that what you have is who you are.*

10. *You are always trying to convince yourself that you got what you want.*

Now carefully consider the following. *When You Want What Life Wants:*

1. *You are never disappointed with what happens.*

2. *You are always in the right place at the right time.*

3. *You are quietly confident no matter what the circumstances.*

4. *You are out of the reach of anger and anxiety.*

5. *You are awake and sensitive to your surroundings.*

6. *You are free of ever feeling as though you've missed out.*

7. *You are never thrown for a loss.*

8. *You are in total command of events.*

9. *You are mentally quiet.*

10. *You are eternally grateful.*

"Is there a simple guideline to follow when it comes to distinguishing between what Life wants and what I want? How can I easily tell which is which?"

"Always remember the following. If any want is the source of anxiety or sorrow, that want is *yours* and not *Life's*. If the want has pain, it is in vain. To let Real Life flood in, pull yourself out of the flood of self-wants that promise a future pleasure but only deliver a *present* pain."

"How do I pull myself out of the flood of my own wants?"

"*See* that you are being washed away by them and you will grow tired of being bounced along. Here is a key. Never accept the presence of any mental or emotional suffering as necessary, no matter how much importance these impostors lend to a particularly pressing want. By refusing their dark presence, you make space for the real Present. This is where the Life you want and that wants you is waiting."

"All of what you have said makes good sense. To tell the truth, I would like to let go and let Life lead, but I'm afraid. What will happen to me if I give up my demands? Won't I lose control of my life."

"You cannot lose control of something you never had control over in the first place. No human being controls life — his or hers or anyone else's. If it weren't for higher cosmic energy coming down and filling your body right now, you couldn't be holding this book in your hands or reading its words. If you want to measure the level of an individual's stress, measure his insistence that life does as he wants. The only thing you will lose by learning to *want what life wants* is your fear of not being in control — which was never real control in the first place but only the sensation of it born out of living with its painful opposite."

Here is the most important point of all. No human being needs control over life because, in reality, no one is apart from it. Who you really are, your True Nature, is not separate from life.

Let Life bring you itself. Welcome it. At each instant, it is new, full — untouched and undiminished by any moment before it. To enter into this full relationship with Life is to give yourself to your Self. Fulfilling the true purpose of Life is fulfilling yourself. They are one and the same. Want What Life Wants.

CHAPTER 6

Break Through to a Totally New You

Starting life over again is the key to a New You. Never mind all of those thoughts and feelings that may be telling you this is impossible — those inner-whisperings that either deny the need for this Self-Newness or that scoff at its possibility. Brush them away with the following helpful insight: Self-defeat in the past does not prove that Self-Victory doesn't exist. Defeat of any kind shows only that you have approached the challenge incorrectly. The only thing a thousand failed attempts to start your life over prove is that you just started in the wrong place a thousand times.

The fact is a New Life does exist. You need only to start looking in the right place. If you are standing over a buried treasure, all you have to do is dig until you find it. If you aren't in the right place, it doesn't matter how hard or how deep you dig, you will come up with nothing except your conviction that there is no treasure. This is where Truth Teachings become so valuable for us. Their unwavering insight into our current level of understanding shows us exactly where we have been trying to succeed with methods that must fail. Listen to these Higher Lessons now and let them reveal the real secrets for breaking through to a New You.

Let Higher Facts Free You from a Painful Past

Starting life over is something we must do every second. We must not wait until we want to start over because at that point wanting to start life over is only our futile wish to avoid what has already happened. Do you remember the lessons from an earlier chapter, in which we learned that we are tied to whatever we avoid? Trying to start our life over because we want to get away from our sad-self — or the sorry situations it has created — is like leaping onto a sinking ship to get off of a collapsing dock. Clearly, this is the way to go under, not to start over. But there *is* a way.

In order to let go of any painful past condition — so there is never again a moment where regret or sorrow is pulling us down — we must allow every movement, each unexpected event encountered, every thought and feeling — no matter its character — to *have its own life*. If we will attempt to view life from this new and higher understanding — that everything under the sun, from thoughts to thunder, has its own birth, life and death — then one day we will come to the relief-filled realization that the reason any part of our painful past persists is because there is something in us that won't let it die out naturally. Any lingering sadness is an unnatural life-form kept breathing by the false self's reluctance to let it go. We can prove this to ourselves and we will; but there is also an abundance of help waiting and available to encourage us on our way.

Physicists have just recently confirmed what religious scholars, wise men and mystics have known all along. Every present moment is always new and new is always right now. Now is constantly shedding the old. The new dies to the ever-new in an endless celebration of Life. This is not philosophy or a misplaced wish for a kinder, gentler universe. Life works through this process. You need only observe any living system to see the beauty and significance of starting over —over and over and over. If anything in life fails to shed the old, it quickly stagnates. A spring that stops replenishing its new waters soon turns dank and sour. This powerful principle is never so true as when it pertains to human life. It is a scientific fact that the *you* who is reading this sentence right now will not be the same *you* that finishes it!

So, the evidence is conclusive. What it tells us is there is no *real* reason why our lives should ever seem stale or feel futile because *real* Life, of which we are a part, is always new right now. This is the fact of it. Our task is to unleash the power of this fact in our own lives. You may be thinking, "What's it going to take for me to break through to totally Present Living? How can I learn to really start over all of the time?"

Just as a weary rock climber must at times reach above himself to gain a difficult resting ledge, you too must dare to go beyond yourself to find this ever-present safety. There is no danger in true self-ascent. The only real danger lies within remaining where you are. Think about it. If you could realize and enter into that true quality of life where there is an entirely New You every moment, it would mean that with every single heartbeat you would be free from any possible heartache that might have preceded it. In this New Life, every relationship begins for the first time over and over again. Every discouragement is over right now. Every challenge, every difficulty is shouldered only in its time and is *never* carried forward or looked back upon with regret. Isn't that what all of us really want? Yes it is!

Do you see what has happened? Something wonderful has already taken place. Our question is no longer, "Is this Ever-New Life really possible?" Now we are asking, "What is it within me that has kept me from living in this new way?" What a difference! If you will only persist with this kind of bold self-questioning, nothing in the universe can stop you from leaving the painful past behind and breaking through to a New You. This is Truth's wondrous promise.

You Are So Much More Than You Can Think

In our quest for the truly new experience of a New Life, we often confuse excitement for true Self-Newness. We want one thing and get the other. Excitement is not newness, any more than getting a shock is the same as getting a boost in life. Somewhere within us our order for a new life is getting turned around. It's like asking for ice cream and the waiter bringing you a grapefruit. At some point you begin to suspect there is someone in the kitchen with his own ideas of what a sweet life is all about.

You are going to have to take things into your own hands. You know that it will probably be frowned upon and that you really don't want to go through the extra trouble. But at some point — because you rarely get what you have asked for — you know you are going to have to go back into the great "kitchen" of life and see for yourself why things just don't come out right. Do it! Your effort will be rewarded far beyond your greatest expectations. The following short story will illustrate this special idea.

A man once wanted a new pair of shoes, so he decided to go to the grand opening of a large department store that had just moved into his neighborhood. When he arrived, it was packed with people waiting to get in. At 9 a.m. the doors opened and he found himself being carried along by the frenzied crowd. Fortunately, a few minutes later, the tide of shoppers had brought him to what appeared to be the shoe department. He looked around and, not seeing any salesperson, he picked up a pair of shoes to try on.

Something must be wrong, he thought to himself, after he had slipped them on. The shoes felt unstable on his feet. He took them off and, upon closer examination, saw that the heels of both shoes were already worn down on one side. He picked up another pair and tried them on. These were very nice looking, but as he stood there he could feel the chill of the tile floor right through the soles. He took the shoes off and inspected them up close. Sure enough, the leather soles of these shoes were almost completely worn through. That was enough. He took the shoes and marched over in his stocking feet to a nearby cashier and demanded to know why this brand-new store would sell such inferior merchandise. The cashier looked at him, smiled patiently, and said, "Sir, this is the section of the store where we only sell previously owned clothing. If it's new shoes you wish to buy you must go up one floor to the new shoe department. I'm sure you'll find what you're looking for up there."

As with all Truth Tales, this little story teaches us several practical and higher lessons all at once. Just as you must be certain of being in the right place when you wish to buy an item of choice, so must you *live from the right part of yourself* if you really wish to find what is authentically new. This is not too difficult to understand. In fact, the real difficulty in life is born out of not understanding these principles.

Remember how we learned in chapter 4 that emotions are something you *feel,* not something you *are?* The same holds true when it comes to your *thinking.* Just as who you *really* are must not be limited or defined by your present feelings, neither must you look for who you really are in your *thoughts* about yourself. Let me show you the self-liberating truth of this amazing idea with a simple example. Once all of this becomes clear to you, staying true to what is new will be as simple as staying true to yourself — which will become your single greatest pleasure in life.

When we think of a lemon, we know that the thought lemon isn't a lemon itself. And yet, if we really think about the lemon, picture it in our mind, our mouth will start watering. Now, even though our mouth may be starting to pucker and we may be having vivid lemon experiences, this still doesn't mean that the *thought* of a lemon is a lemon. All that has happened is the thought "lemon" triggered a series of unconscious accumulated memories which rushed to our awareness producing all of the different sensations connected with things that are lemon-like. Presto! The thought lemon *appears* to be real because just the thought of it produces temporary but definite feelings that are connected to things yellow or tart.

This is an easy concept to grasp when it comes to lemons since not too many of us are painfully identified with lemons. We are talking about what it means to *identify*. When you think that who you are is connected to something you are not, you have identified with it. To make this clear, think about how you felt the last time you accidentally scuffed your brand-new shoes or tore your brand-new pants. It felt like it was *you* who got damaged! Remember? That's what it means to be identified with something or someone. It hurts! None of this is too difficult to understand when it comes to things outside of us; but, when it comes to the word "I," suddenly the mental fog rolls in. Let me repeat the beginning of this lesson. You are not who you think you are. Now let's consider this important idea using what we have just learned about identification.

When you think of yourself, when you say the word "I," the same series of inner-movements surround and support this "I" as happened earlier when you thought about the word lemon. Only each time you think of this "I," your "self," there is even a greater storehouse of accumulated memories and experiences that rush forth forming an *almost* solid wall of thoughts and feelings. In that moment of thinking about your "self," you *feel* real because as these waves of your accumulated past wash through you, it gives you the *feeling* of being you; but this feeling is only a temporary condition. No matter how many times or how strongly you may feel it, *this sensation of "I" is not you.* You are not your past. You have only become unconsciously identified with it at that moment. It is your identification with these sensations that provides you with a convincing, but nevertheless temporary, sense of self. This false identity, this false self as we have been calling it, is false because *it is a borrowed life;* it is derived from something that in itself is only temporary.

The great playwright and philosopher, William Shakespeare, wrote, "Neither a borrower nor a lender be for a loan oft loses both itself and friend." How much more so does this powerful idea hold when it comes to Life itself? The Truth tells us that we must never borrow anything — let alone our Identity. No wonder life seems to have lost that vibrant quality of being new every moment. We only thought we were living a Real Life! Trying to find and own your True Self while living in and from this borrowed, counterfeit identity is like waiting for the sun to come out in a deep, subterranean cave. There is lots of excited anticipation but none of the light and warmth that come with true self-realization.

Drop Angry and Anxious Feelings Instantly

In order to have a sunny life on a moment-to-moment basis, you must be willing to let something new happen to you. No one sincerely asks for a new life until they are thoroughly dissatisfied with the old one. Letting go of the old ideas is the only way to *really* invite something new. This is what we are learning to do with the help of these higher ideas. Let's look at one example of how our new self-knowledge can turn a painful and repetitive unhappiness into a bright and positive new experience.

Imagine that someone you think of as a friend suddenly becomes very disagreeable towards you. This could be at home or at work. The location and circumstances do not matter. We all know what happens. First, there is the initial confrontation. Then, either in a bang or like a kettle steadily building pressure, your friend begins expressing these angry and steamy feelings. Now you too are starting to boil. But, you have been studying yourself. And, because you have been practicing higher self-observation, the arrival of these hot feelings brings with it more than just fire; there is also a new light. And in this special inner-light you can see that the surfacing anger is born out of being identified with feelings of fear; fear that this person before you doesn't understand you, might leave you, has stopped "caring," or will no longer serve to confirm your point of view. In past situations such as these, prior to the awakening of this higher self-awareness, you would have gone on heating up and probably gone off yourself. There would have been yet another self-explosion and more people, including yourself, would have hated their day. However, that is not the case this time.

Why? Because instead of defending your position as was your old habit, you now understand that this "you" who is feeling threatened or attacked is not who you really are. You know your true nature never needs to defend any psychological or emotional position. This higher knowledge, along with your wish to let something new happen, allows you to simply and instantly drop this reactionary and false identity. Congratulations! At the instant you dropped this false life, you momentarily merged with the Real Life. Here's the explanation. By starting your life over in that moment — by *not* borrowing your life from a heated reaction — you let that negative fear-feeling live and *die*. When you allowed yourself to let go of what was old, you stayed true to what is new.

The benefits of this clear-cut new and true action are many. Just one of them is that you don't have to go on living with the angry or anxious feelings that always accompany the insistence that others see life as you do.

Here are five life-liberating insights that will help you to let something new happen in your life. You will see as with all real insights, higher understanding itself contains not only the instructions you must follow but the strength you will need to carry them out. Go over these following ideas with the intent of receiving their hidden message.

1

Self-doubt *is born out of being identified with the idea that how you feel about yourself depends upon how others feel about you. Give up self-doubt. It only makes you more dependent on others who can't do anything about their own self-doubt. Independence is confidence.*

2

Self-righteousness *is born out of being identified with the idea that just because you can point out something that is wrong places you above that wrongness. Give up the self-righteousness. It only feels like something right. It is coming from something that is wrong. Right isn't something you feel. It is something you are.*

3

Self-pity *and past regrets are born out of being identified with the idea that you could have done differently than you did. If you could have, you would have. Give up the regret. It only ties you to the old life-level that didn't know better and keeps you from the one that does.*

4

Anger *is born out of being identified with the fear you feel when others won't conform to your point of view. Give up your anger towards others and yourself by seeing that the force of fear is not strength. Remember that for any and every action of force there is an equal and opposite one. This explains why the fighting never ends. Let it end.*

5

Self-torment *is born out of being identified with the idea that the more you suffer the more real, the more important, you must be. Give up all self-torment. It drives you — but it doesn't take you anywhere. Who you really are never suffers over who it isn't.*

Giving Yourself Up Is Lifting Yourself Up

The gradual realization that you need never again try to find yourself in your thoughts about yourself is like one day happily realizing that hitting yourself over the head was the cause and not the cure for your daily headaches. To your grateful amazement, you discover that the inner-pounding you so wished would go away finally came to a stop when *you* stopped pounding. This startling realization brings you to a crucial moment in your quest for self-newness. And you must be resolute. As you begin to suspend your habitual involvement with yourself — which you know you must do in order to let something new happen — you begin to notice an altogether different kind of disturbing feeling starting to rise up within you. You would never have believed it, but there it is right in front of your inner-eyes. You are actually beginning to worry about what is going to happen to you without your worry. Nothing doing! You instantly catch and drop this fake feeling along with the rest of the inner-impostors. They want you to believe that there might not be life without suffering. And yet, even with all of this clear to your inner-eyes, you are still tempted for a moment to drop your inner-vigilance. Anything seems better than this increasing self-uncertainty. Don't mistake these feelings of fear for friends. Listen instead to what the Truth is trying to tell you.

Have no concern whatsoever over where these feelings of unknowing will lead you. The seemingly intelligent self-concern over your rising feelings of vulnerability is nothing but another false identity. Suspend it as well. Deny its re-entrance into your life. This total suspension of self allows the present moment to flood in unfiltered and uncolored. Something genuinely new is happening and you *know* it. This newness is your true home. Within it you are safe and out of the reach and grip of familiar but fierce self-creating thoughts and feelings. Persist with this higher kind of self-suspension for as long as it takes until slowly, but surely, you feel the weighted drag of your habitual self less and less. As you grow lighter in spirit, you will see that this Newness you have fought for is who you really are. Here lies your True Nature. It was there all along — like the strong, unshakable shelter of a deep mountainside cave you were at first afraid to enter when caught off guard by a fierce storm. To your everlasting delight, you find within this special kind of newness true refuge. In its strength yours is renewed. All is well. The storms can no longer reach you.

Here is a special exercise that can help you to start letting go of yourself. Every time you catch yourself just about to take a swim in the old habitual river of thoughts and feelings, practice *self-suspension.* Here's how. Don't let the current of the past dictate the direction of the present moment. Have your own life right now. You are not your thoughts and feelings. Dare to live without each painful identity that calls for you to embrace it and to do its bidding. *Let something new happen* each moment by letting these old, habitual sensations go their way unobstructed. Stay out of them. Work at this special self-suspension and inner-alertness until the day you find this newness you once had to struggle to endure is now something you could not endure living without!

How to Live Life on Your Own Terms

Did you know that behind each fact is a friendly force? And that's not all. A fact will never let you down or be untrue. There's more. Even though it may at times appear otherwise, facts have total authority over falsehoods. Why? Because a fact is rooted in reality and it draws all the strength it needs to eventually prevail over what is untrue from the fabric of life itself. This is a fact. You can bank on it. Now here is another bankable fact you may not have known. I'm certain you will welcome its life-healing entrance into your life.

No human being has any authority over you. Your life belongs to you and to you alone. *No scowling face or irritated manner, no challenging posture or threatening tone has any power to make you feel nervous or anxious, frightened or angry.* This is a fact; and anyone who is tired of letting someone else tell them how to feel can use this self- liberating principle to win true and lasting independence.

Let's repeat this fundamental fact once more — it is so important to our total mental, emotional and spiritual well-being. No human being has any authority over who you really are. Your true nature answers to no man. What this means is if we are not living life completely on our own terms — if there is anyone in our life that dominates us — it is not, I repeat it is not because life has in some way given that person an unfair advantage or power over us. The fact is simply that we have unknowingly given away our true heritage; a heritage that calls to us now to remind us that our spirit cannot be dominated by anyone or anything. Each of us is entitled to be a wholly independent and totally free human being. The Truth declares that nothing real stands between you and this noble life and then invites you to recover the real pleasure of living life on your own terms.

"I can actually feel the rightness in this declaration and there are times when it seems I am able to live life on my own terms. Then there are those other times when, for some unknown reason, it feels like I have no life of my own. Do you know what I mean?"

"Yes I do. Can you be more specific? There are special benefits whenever you give yourself permission to honestly bring your self-doubts and suspected weaknesses up to the level of conscious awareness."

"All right, I'm willing to try. For instance, I don't understand why I'm afraid to talk to some people; and then there are others with whom I can't stop talking, even though I wish I could. Then sometimes I agree to do things for people I don't really want to do at all, or I find myself in places where I don't really want to be — with people I don't really like — and yet I can't seem to leave. And to be really honest with you, I don't know why sometimes I feel so much resentment toward the very people whose approval means the most to me. It just doesn't make sense. When these times come, not only am I unsure of why I am acting the way I am, but I don't even like myself. It doesn't add up! How can a person be in charge of his own life one minute, and in the next minute find it in someone else's hands? What's going on?

"You're right, it doesn't add up; and the truth is, it never will as long as you are figuring in flattering but false notions about yourself. Plug this new self-insight into your equation and see if things don't immediately make more sense. Whenever you do something that you resent doing but feel compelled to do, you must unconsciously be more concerned with how others feel about you than you are with how you are really feeling. This is what it means to live in conflict."

"I can see this must be the case. It explains almost everything except for why I would want to treat myself this way. Why, especially in light of these new facts, do I care at all about how I appear in the eyes of others?"

"Please follow this explanation carefully. It will set you back on the road to having your own life. You have always believed that the better people feel about you, the better you can feel about yourself. However, you may have never really considered that the opposite of this belief must hold equally and unhappily true, and that is: The less you are approved by others, the more alone and uncertain you feel. This helps to explain why you think you have to please people as well as why you resent those you feel you must please. Being approved by others has become a strange kind of life-support system wherein, after a lifetime of depending on it, you unconsciously believe that there won't be life without someone there to approve you into existence. Just the opposite is true. The more you depend on others to confirm you to yourself, the less real life you have of your own."

"Yes, but surely you aren't saying that there is anything wrong with receiving the approval of others?"

"No, of course not. It occurs spontaneously and healthfully in any natural human relationship. However, we are discovering that there is a vast difference between winning and *seeking* approval. We must be very alert to the whole process of peer approval. Cunning human beings understand just how deep and strong run the forces that drive us to look for approval from others. They use this knowledge of our weakness for their own gain. Only higher self-awareness which produces active inner-alertness can keep us safe from these unconscious and misguided self-betraying forces — as well as from those who would use them against us."

"Who would have ever guessed this problem would be so deep?"

"Listen to me. It is not deep. It's just not clear to you yet. Imagine a murky countryside pond. It could have a depth of several fathoms or it could be just knee deep. Inner difficulties only *seem* deep because our false nature keeps everything so stirred up inside of us that we can't see to the real bottom of them. The purpose of truthful ideas is to clear things up. When we are inwardly quiet and can see ourselves clearly, we can wade through our difficulties without any fear of being in over our heads. Once we can see the cause of a problem, we know its solution."

"I like that illustration. Please continue."

"Yes, let's see how all of this connects. We have learned it is our fear of being alone and in doubt, of wanting to feel certain that what we are doing is right, that compels us to seek the approval of others. So this tells us the chief cause of why our lives so often wind up in the hands of others is not that they are superior or that the world is too strong for us, but that we don't want to face the uncertainty and aloneness we think we are too weak to bear. This is the *real* cause of all of our wrong relationships in life. *We have been betrayed by a belief in our own weakness.*"

"This is great! I think I'm ahead of you. Then the solution must be to refuse to go along with the weakness?"

"Yes! The conscious refusal to go along with your weakness is what invokes and finally delivers real inner-strength. This new kind of strength gradually becomes the cornerstone of a true individual existence — the life you've always wanted. The stakes are actually eternal — but self-victory is as certain as the fact that light always triumphs over darkness. If you will stay in the middle of this struggle for true self-possession, not asserting your individuality but allowing it to flourish and to blossom — bearing what you must bear by refusing to submit yourself to negative, self-betraying influences — you will come to know the highest approval that life can award. Reality itself will approve you. And when it does, all of your struggles will become a thing of the past. You will possess yourself. No one around you will suspect you now live in a new kind of bright inner-world; a world that is always on your terms because your terms and the terms of this happy new inner-world are never in conflict. You have won your own life."

Special study section for lasting self-possession:

1

When you don't know what to do with yourself, someone will always be happy to tell you.

2

Why seek the approval of someone who doesn't even approve of himself?

3

Fawning before an angry person is like asking a rabid wolf for its approval.

4

The more approval you get, the more you have to have.

5

Keeping any person or circumstance in your life that demands you surrender your right to be a whole and happy human being is wrong for everyone *involved.*

6

When you are out standing in a storm, don't blame the weather.

7

Real strength always follows uncovering one of the roots of weakness.

8

Don't seek *yourself. Dare to* be *yourself.*

9

If you were really *doing the right thing with your life, you wouldn't need anyone to tell you that you were.*

10

Permitting your life to be taken over by another person is like letting the waiter eat your dinner.

(Vernon Howard)

Ask Yourself This Question and Escape to Freedom

An evil sorcerer once hypnotized a group of captives into believing that whatever he wanted was what they wanted. It was a powerful black spell. Not only did it keep each of his psychic slaves unconscious to his own unhappy feelings, but it also made him believe that he had no choice but to feel that way.

And so these poor men and women worked willingly for the sorcerer even though they were often commanded to act in ways that made them go against their own true nature. Year after year they went on hurting one another as they continued to toil unknowingly under the evil influence of his cruel spell. Then, one day, right in the middle of carrying out one of the sorcerer's wicked wishes, one of the captives had a startling insight. It came to him like a bolt of lightning. He wondered why he had never before thought to ask himself such a simple question. Here is what he wondered even as he was struggling to complete his unpleasant appointed task.

"If I am doing what I want to do, how come it hurts me to do it?" There was no way for him to know it right then, but this seemingly unimportant question was the beginning of a great miracle that would one day allow him to command his own life once again.

From that point on, every day and every time he would find himself unexplainably unhappy he would ask himself this same question: If I am doing what I want to do, how come it hurts *me* to do it? What he didn't know was that each time he asked this of himself, he was, at that same moment, delivering a smashing blow to the hold of the sorcerer's evil spell. Soon the happy day arrived when he just couldn't find any more good reason, *in his own mind,* to go on hurting himself. This final realization spelled the end of the evil influence in his life. He escaped his unhappy existence and fled home to freedom.

No one really wants to talk about it, but the truth is there is a kind of evil spell hanging over each of us and our world as well. In fact, part of this global spell is our denial of its existence. It is called suffering. Everyone does it — and like the hypnotized captives in our story — everyone believes that their suffering somehow benefits them. That's how the spell works. Why else would anyone punish himself with unhappy feelings unless he had been tricked into somehow perceiving self-hurt as self-help?

Let's examine one of these instances. First of all, to be angry *is* to suffer. It doesn't help anyone to get angry. Anger hurts whoever is angry. It burns. Anger ruins relationships, causes heartache and regret, and devastates health. And yet, in spite of all of these facts, when we are angry it feels right. Somehow, in some unseen way, anger proves to whoever is experiencing its heated feelings that he or she is right even though, in the eyes of reality, nothing could be further from the truth. The same scenario holds true of worry, anxiety, resentment, doubt, guilt or any dark feeling. How can something so wrong seem so right? Here is the answer. All of these negative emotions *feel* like they are in your best interest because, at the time of their intrusion into your life, they temporarily fill you with a powerful false sense of self. However, just like the sorcerer's evil spell in our story, this sense of self born out of fierce but lying feelings can only exist *without* your conscious consent or awareness of its being there. Why? Because this negative-self's interests are not in *your* best interest. This conjured-up temporary identity is nothing but a self-of-suffering. No one chooses to lose.

This lesson may seem difficult at first, but with your persistent wish to understand it, you will one day wonder how you were ever tricked into feeling bad about anything. The Truth wants you to know that it is *never* in your best interest to suffer, no matter how inwardly convincing it may feel to you that you will be betraying yourself or someone else if you don't. The only way that any suffering feeling can prove to you that you need it is to hypnotize you with a flood of itself. Step back from yourself. Learn instead to listen to the quiet stream of higher insight that runs softly through your true nature. It sees through sorrow. Let it show you that suffering proves nothing. If you want to receive some special help for helping yourself escape yourself, always remember the key question that freed the hypnotized hero in our story. It freed him from his psychic captivity and it will do the same for you. I'll repeat it for you. "If I am doing what I want to do, then how come it hurts *me* to do it?" The truth guarantees you will stop doing what you don't want to do once you *know* what you have been doing against yourself.

Step Up and Away from Punishing Feelings

Here are ten powerful ways to snap the spell of suffering. As you read over each one, think about how you can use its insight the next time you are about to be washed by any flood of painful thoughts or feelings. Welcome their higher influence into your life.

1

Suffering doesn't prove that you know what it means to care about yourself or others. What it does prove is you haven't seen through your own ideas about caring or you wouldn't be so careless with yourself.

2

Suffering doesn't prove that you are right. What it does prove is you don't really know right from wrong or you wouldn't take your position of pain as your proof of point.

3

Suffering doesn't prove that you are responsible. What it does prove is you have abandoned true self-responsibility, or you wouldn't treat yourself so badly.

4

Suffering doesn't prove that you are important. What it does prove is you would rather feel like a "someone" who is miserable than be a "no one" who is free and quietly happy.

5

Suffering doesn't prove that you are all alone in life. What it does prove is you prefer the company of unfriendly thoughts and feelings whose very nature is to isolate you from everything good.

6

Suffering doesn't prove that the world is against you. What it does prove is you have taken sides with that which is against everything — including yourself.

7

Suffering doesn't prove that you are real. *What it does prove is you have identified with an agitated false feeling of life and confused it for the quiet fullness of Real Living.*

8

Suffering doesn't prove that someone else is wrong. What it does prove is you will go to any lengths, including self-destruction, to prove that you are right.

9

Suffering doesn't prove that you are who you think you are. What it does prove is you don't know who you really *are or you would never tolerate a suffering-self as an identity.*

10

Suffering over your suffering doesn't prove that you want to stop suffering. What it does prove is you are afraid of the end of suffering because you think the end of it means the end of you. It does not.

Each newly gained higher insight presents a unique challenge when we first glimpse its existence. We must proceed just like a dedicated mountain climber who first spots a previously unknown and seemingly unreachable peak. He is at once attracted to its majesty and excited by the promise of its lofty secrets, but reluctant to begin his ascent because he knows it will be difficult. However, his love of the climb outweighs his fear of falling and so he brushes away the last thought of difficulty. He understands all he needs to do to reach the new heights is to study the slope and then start to climb. He knows better than to be fooled by his heavy, discouraging feelings that never want him to go higher. He knows each ascent is taken one step at a time.

The same holds true for the inner-ascent. First we learn the facts, study higher ideas, then we start the climb. *Whatever is true can be reached.* It is true that you need never suffer. Here is an exercise to help you take the first step up and away from self-punishing feelings.

This exercise is called: *Is This What I Really Want?*

You do not have to accept *any* inner-condition that compromises your happiness. Read over the next sentence several times before proceeding further. It is never right to feel wrong no matter how right you may *think* you are to be feeling that way. *Feeling* one way and *thinking* another is what it means to live in conflict. Self-conflict is really the only suffering there is; therefore, self-unity is the only real solution that can snap the spell of self-suffering.

Here is how it works. The next time you catch yourself starting to feel bad about anything, immediately stop everything you are doing for a moment and, as simply and as honestly as you can, ask yourself: *Is this what I really want?* Try to see the whole self-picture as it is unfolding. You will discover that your *thoughts* are convinced that you must proceed in *their* direction of worry or revenge or fear but *you* are the one who is feeling bad. These self-betraying thoughts are like a friend who invites you out to a pleasant evening at the fights and then you find yourself in the ring as the main event! I repeat, you do not have to accept *any* condition that compromises your happiness.

You can and must inwardly say to any conflicting thoughts or feelings that, "You are not what I want!" The clearer this whole picture becomes to you — that suffering is stupid and must *never* be justified — the stronger your right self-assertion for self-unity will become. A whole life is a happy one. Choose to have a happy life by choosing what *you* really want.

Make It All the Way Home to Your True Self

Ask someone who he is and he will probably tell you where he lives, what he does, how others see him, as well as how he sees himself; and then he will go on to tell you his detailed plans to eventually improve on everything he has just told you. This person makes the same mistake that all of us make when it comes to the age-old question of "Who am I?" He is looking for himself in all the wrong places. He is desperately trying to find himself in the eyes of family, friends or lovers, in his achievements, successes or hobbies, or in traditional religious beliefs or spiritual principles; and when all of these roads fail to lead him to a safe and secure self — which they could never do in the first place — he then mistakenly seeks himself in the self-slashing feelings of fear, despair, anxiety or defeat. It may not be much, but desperation is incapable of discernment and so even an identity to loath is better than none at all. This kind of self-abandonment does two things for him.

First, it fills the space that rushes in when he doesn't find himself in his usual ideas or when life won't confirm his self-pictures. In his desperation for finding himself, he accepts *anything* that fills the gap. Secondly, his distaste for himself at this moment is so great that it supplies him with a powerful motivation to get away from this unwanted, unhappy self. His nightmare is that he only *thinks* he escapes this sorrowful-self because he always returns to seeking himself in the same kind of places and faces. Since nothing has really changed, he must eventually recreate this painful pattern again . . . and again. This is not life.

Who you really are, your True Original Self, is not a creation of your self. You can think yourself into a self of doubt and fear, but you cannot think yourself into security or real happiness. Stop worrying about who you think you should be and start being who you are. How? Stop telling yourself who you *should* be and start listening for an altogether new kind of voice that has been quietly calling to you. Let it show you where to find your Self. Here is an inner-life tale about a courageous cub that will help you capture the higher points of this chapter.

The infant animal didn't know where he was or how he got there. He wasn't even that sure about what he was. Everything was so confused. His mind raced with questions. How did he get here and what should he do? Which direction should he take and, most importantly, who and where was his family? If he could just get that straightened out, maybe the rest would take care of itself. To make things worse, if that was possible, the only thing noisier than his own chattering mind was the jungle treetops that were filled with the excited voices of hundreds of unusual creatures.

"No sense just waiting here," he thought to himself, and he began to walk cautiously toward a group of animals he could see just across a small clearing of recently toppled trees. As he drew nearer he comforted himself thinking, "Maybe these are my brothers and sisters."

In a flash, one of the larger animals rushed out to evaluate the youngster as friend or foe. Fortunately, after a tense moment or two, the dominant female baboon accepted him and, soon after, the whole tribe took him in as one of their own. That was how he felt too. At least for a while.

He learned to groom and to be groomed and to climb trees and rocks. However, after a little while, he started feeling very unhappy. He didn't care for their manners at all. Their incessant and totally meaningless chattering gave him a constant headache. But worse than that was how unbelievably nervous and jumpy all of them were most all of the time. Finally he made up his mind he had to leave. This simply could not be where he belonged.

After a short while of wandering along a narrow riverbed, he spied something that made his spirits brighten. Ahead of him was a small group of fearless animals. Their bravery was tremendous. They were fighting over possession of a waterhole with some larger, hideous sounding animal.

"Here," he thought, "are my family at last," and he jumped into the battle on their side.

The warthogs were even more surprised than the embattled hyena. Clearly overmatched, the hyena fled and soon, after some snorting and other strange behavior, the warthogs accepted the obviously confused youngster into their ranks. He lived with them for a while, but again it wasn't long before he knew something was terribly wrong. First of all, he couldn't stand using his nose to dig in the ground for grubs. It hurt! And then there was their endless snorting. Whenever he tried to talk their way, it always came out wrong. Mostly, though, he was very uncomfortable with how touchy everyone was and how, amongst their own kind, fights were much more the rule than was tenderness. He didn't want to leave, but he knew in his heart this wasn't where he belonged. It wasn't an easy choice. And as he walked away his mind kept telling him that if he left this newest family of his, he would be by himself forever. He had never felt so strangely alone. Even the endless jungle sounds couldn't fill the emptiness he was feeling.

He walked on for quite a while without noticing the scenery around him was changing dramatically. Little by little, the surroundings went from dense trees to open spaces. A few times he saw other groups of animals, but he didn't bother to stop and see if they were his own. Somehow he just instinctively knew better. At a certain point he stopped to rest. As he lay there quietly looking at all of the life going on around him, he couldn't help but notice a strange feeling going on within him. Try as he might, he couldn't explain it to himself. After all, he shouldn't be feeling so good! And yet, that was exactly how he felt.

"How could this be?" he wondered. "I don't have any idea who I am or even where I belong. All I have found so far is who I am not."

It was right in the middle of this thought that there came a sound from across the plain that made his heart come to a jolting stop. He had never heard such power in the voice of any animal. Again it rolled over the plain — right up to and straight through him. He wanted to run but, as crazy as it was, he didn't know whether to run away from these disturbing sounds or toward them. Finally he had no choice. He ran in the direction of the roaring. The closer he got to the small band of regal-appearing animals, the more certain he began to feel that somehow he had found his home. He opened his mouth to greet everyone and out of him came the same powerful roar. His heart leapt. He had found his own. He was and had always been the King of the Jungle. Now, he knew it. He was home.

Here is a grand summary of this chapter section that will help you in your search to find out who you really are. Dare to walk away from all of the familiar but useless mental and emotional relationships that give you a temporary but unsatisfactory self. Your true identity is calling to you. But to hear it you must be willing to endure, for as long as necessary, the fear of self-uncertainty. This form of seeming self-abandonment eventually turns into your greatest pleasure as it becomes increasingly evident that the only thing certain about fear is that it will *always* compromise you. When it comes to who you really are, there is *no* compromise.

Here is a great mystery. Only when you know who you are *not* will you know who *you really are*. Listen for the call of your Royal Nature. Don't be afraid of open spaces. Seek the Truth, not security. You too will make it all the way home to your True Self.

CHAPTER 7

Let Go and Let Higher Life Forces Succeed for You

Have you ever looked down at a sidewalk or parking lot and marveled at a single blade of grass that had somehow found the will and the way to break through the pavement out into the fresh air and sunlight? When we think of a titanic struggle, we don't usually think of a little seed of grass buried in the darkness and fighting to get out in the light. And yet, even though we may not see it as we hurry through our days, this ancient struggle for life in the light that goes on just beneath our feet is actually taking place within us as well. Mostly unanswered but endlessly calling to each and every one of us is our natural and Higher Need to find our place in the sun; a world just outside of our old limited self where Real Life is open and free. This need in each of us to rise above ourselves is an Eternal Law that expresses itself in all living things.

However, unlike the new grass or mustard seed which seeks the sunlight with no concern for what may be blocking its way, we are often easily discouraged by the host of inner-shadows that stand between us and a bright new life. This is an unhappy condition that only grows sadder each time we fight and fail to free ourselves. That's why we must learn how to fight right. This right kind of self-understanding is everything if we wish to win. Here's how it applies to discovering the wondrous world outside of yourself. If your quest for self-freedom has been repeatedly rejected, it isn't because you have lacked the strength or opportunity. Neither the abundance nor the absence of these circumstantial attributes makes any real difference when it comes to true self-escape.

The wise eagle knows just where to wait on the wing for certain powerful updrafts. Its compliance with natural laws is rewarded with a soaring life. So we too must learn to comply with the higher laws that govern self-liberation if we wish to be lifted. That is what this book is all about.

For now, let's see how these natural laws govern even the smallest of things. Jesus Christ spoke of these compassionate Higher Principles when he said, "Consider the lilies, how they grow: They toil not. They spin not; and yet I say to you, that Solomon in all his glory was not arrayed like one of these. If God so clothe the grass, which is today in the field and tomorrow is cast into the oven, how much more will he clothe you, 0 ye of little faith?" If these Higher Principles take such astonishing care with the least in life, how much more so are they capable of helping those who choose to cooperate with their immutable laws?

We know that a young shoot of grass born in the darkness must soon break out into the warming rays of the sun; otherwise it will perish. It must get outside of its present unfavorable circumstances in order to claim its full life. Of course, this tender little shoot of new life can't know this, but it is not alone in its desperate fight for the light. In its favor is LIFE itself — an intelligent and undeniable force that meets all barriers with the same fearlessness. And so the baby grass emerges against all odds because Life, in one way or another, invariably finds a way to be stronger than anything that would deny it the expression of itself.

You can have these same powerful Life Forces working for you. Surely you have felt the need for a greater life outside of yourself. Who hasn't? We all feel this natural need for rising above self-limiting thoughts and feelings because our True Nature, like the source of Light that it is, beckons to us to emerge out from under the heaviness of our own mistaken false identity. It wants to give us a New Life in exchange for our old one. It asks only that we willingly comply with its eternal process of self-renewal and it does the rest.

Don't wonder whether or not this is true. You can see it for yourself. The proof you seek is in every living thing around you. There is a new world of lightness and rightness just outside of your present self. The journey can be made. Others have gone before you.

Crash Through These Self-Confining Thoughts

Truth teachings are given as instructions and encouragement for you to allow Real Life to come in and move you up and away from your old nature. True self-development should be as natural for human beings as it is for flowers to turn their faces to the sun. However, there is much we haven't as yet understood about real spiritual life and much we think we know which we don't. The following short story by Vernon Howard is from his book Inspire Yourself. It is one of my favorite Truth tales because it is full of higher hints about our unseen inner-condition as well as what is asked of us if we want to make it outside of our present unpleasant self-confinement. It is called, "The Bewildered Metal."

> *A strip of metal once rested comfortably on a low shelf in a factory. It remained there for a long time, doing nothing but collecting dust.*

One day a workman picked it up, carried it to a bench, and began to twist it out of its usual shape. 'Why are you doing this to me?' shouted the alarmed and frightened strip of metal.

'To enable you to see wonders beyond your imagination,' replied the workman. 'Just now it all seems strange and frightening, but some day you will be very glad. You see, I am turning you into a telescope.'

A WILLINGNESS TO PASS THROUGH INNER CHANGE ENABLES US TO SEE THE VASTNESS BEYOND OUR PRESENT POSITION.[1]

The key to leaving behind our self-created and self-limited world is to be found in our willingness to *keep going*, even when it "feels" like something bad is happening to us or that we're going "nowhere fast." The idea of quitting or turning back is the unfortunate option that occurs only when we have an incomplete understanding of any given situation. This is where Higher Knowledge becomes so important for our real inner-progress. When you know in your heart that you must keep going but your feet just aren't getting the message, self-understanding can open and carry you through doors that self-insistence cannot. Here's how.

Through our self studies we know that the false self must find a way to convince us that its world is the only world. One of the ways it accomplishes this mean feat is by talking to us through sinister inner-voices. These talking thoughts can be heard whispering or crying out:

"What's the use?"

"You're not making any progress!"

"You've tried to change but life is just too tough."

1Vernon Howard, *Inspire Yourself.* (New Life, 1975).

"Why rock the boat?"

"Just go back to your old ways. It'll be a lot easier."

In these and other equally devious ways, the false self tries to pass its frightened and change-resistant thinking off on you as your very own thoughts. These defeated and self-sorry thoughts do not belong to you. They are coming at you from inside the same limited world that Real Life is now inviting you to leave. Your faint but sincere wish to leave your false self behind compels this lower nature to do everything in its power to make you believe that self-exit is not only dangerous but impossible. It knows that the only way it can hope to win this crucial inner battle is to somehow convince you that you have lost. What it doesn't want you to know is that it has no real power of its own to stop you on your appointed journey up and out. That's right! Listen to this amazing fact. The false self and all that makes it up is mechanical in nature. It is made up of dusty memories, ingrained habits, ancient fears, recurring doubts, familiar pleasures and many other reactions of endless variety. In short, the false self is not really alive. It has no more Real Life than does a fifty-cent amusement park ride.

Let the World Inside of You Go By

A man once awakened to find himself riding through what appeared to be a haunted house. He didn't know exactly where he was. All he did know was that it was very dark and that he was moving along with no choice as to the direction. And if that wasn't bad enough, around almost every twisting corner he knew that something out of his worst dreams was ready to leap out at him. He was about to jump out of the car and run for help when he thought he heard a strong quiet voice speaking directly to him.

"Stay in the car," it said, "Don't be afraid. This darkness and its creatures are not real. You don't have to be brave, but if you want out of this scary place, you must wait in the car until the ride is over. If you jump out now, you will just get out into the darkness. Listen to me. The sunlight is just ahead. You don't have to do anything except let the ride end."

He knew something out of the ordinary was happening to him because, right about then, his conventional wisdom would have had him out of the car and running like a wild man for anything that even resembled the way out. In some unexplainable way he sensed he had been in this position before and that this time he must do something altogether new.

And so, instead of listening to his own frantic feelings, he decided in favor of following the strange instructions that had just come to him. Some tense moments that seemed like a lifetime later, he found himself rolling out into the sunlight just as he had been told would happen if he would wait out the ride. To his great relief, it had only been a wild ride after all. Now here is the inner-explanation for this story and chapter section. Ride it all the way to freedom.

Every sustained effort you make to get outside of yourself and to change the kind of human being you are will bring up in you a host of thoughts and feelings that can't wait to point out the negatives as to why this can't be done. We've all heard their whine within. They cry out, "no way," "why try?" "too tough," and on and on it goes. Unexamined, these inner-voices appear to have our best interests in mind. But, if we'll persist in our wish to rise above ourself in spite of all this clamoring, these same resistant reactions will be forced to reveal themselves as the hulking giants of fear and despair that they have always been! They are not your friends. In fact, their only appointed task is to see to it that you turn back. These fierce but fake fiends usually accomplish their task by making you believe that you can't go any further with them blocking the way.

Now comes the best part. Here is the beauty and the Rescue of Higher Self-Knowledge. You don't have to go any further. Just as in the story of the man's scary ride through the haunted house, all you need to do is to listen to the voice of Truth and do what it tells you to do. Listen now. You don't have to do anything about what tries to disturb you on your journey to outside of yourself. In fact, like the man in our story, you mustn't do anything except stay in the "car." You are safe there — in the *awareness* of your fears — and not in running away from one scary doubt right into the arms of another. Practice this new lesson in Higher Self-Patience over and over. Real inner-progress is not measured by what you do with any particular scary thought or feeling, but by your new understanding which now instructs you that there is nothing that needs to be done with it. If you will wait out the "ride" of these frightening thoughts and feelings, they will eventually fade into the nothingness they came out of in the first place. To discover the wondrous world outside of yourself let the world inside of yourself go by. All you need do is your part. Just like sunlight, victory comes to you.

This Higher Instruction Will Take You Beyond Yourself

"To tell you the truth, I think it would be a real relief to get outside of myself but how do I get there? How can I be certain I'm headed in the right direction?"

"Here is a great secret known only by those who have made the journey before you. Follow its Higher Instruction and you will find the success you seek. Walk away from the mental how into the spiritual Now."

This secret instruction deserves our close attention. Its real value, like that of a priceless jewel, is best appreciated when seen from every angle. Just as it is the nature of such a rare jewel to reflect its inner brilliance in all directions, so is it the nature of this new, Higher Instruction to light your way once you have unlocked its secret. Here is one of its keys. The journey outside of yourself doesn't take you to a place, but to the realization that who you really are lives above the world of thoughts and feelings. The everyday mental life which naturally includes asking "how" has its practical place in the world of auto mechanics, building a house or running a computer. These kinds of tasks are governed by the mental life. Living and working in this physical world, it is necessary to ask "how" in order to learn to "do." However, when it comes to learning how to live above and outside of our self, the same mental life that can safely deliver men to the moon cannot take us any higher or further than its loftiest thought! And, as we have already learned, the thought is never the thing. In other words, it is impossible to think your Self outside of yourself.

We are now at an important stage in our self-work. Let's briefly review. We want to know "how" to proceed with our inner-journey, but we now also understand that even the finest mental life cannot deliver us beyond what are its own inherent limitations. From this unique inner-vantage point we can see that something altogether new, some unthinkable leap is needed if we are to successfully bridge the gap between this limited mental world and the New Life we seek beyond our self.

"I'm not certain I'm following. If my thoughts can't lift me above myself, then how do I let go of my present life-level and move to a higher one?"

"As you begin to realize the true restrictions of living from a thought-dominated self, you will no longer ask 'how' because part of your new realization will include the understanding that this habitual question of 'how' to get outside of yourself is actually arising from the same life-level you are trying to leave! At this important stage of your inner-development there may be times when it will seem to you as though there is no way out. It is always helpful to keep in mind that the false self wants you to feel that way. You'll be glad to hear that the Truth has something better for you to do than feeling trapped. Here is its instruction: Each time you reach this inner-point of self-uncertainty where you know you must take a step but you also know that you can no longer ask 'how,' just *go ahead and step forward anyway!* Step into what appears to be the darkness ahead of you. Nothing bad will happen. In fact, something miraculous will occur right before your eyes. Your decision in favor of this bold new action thrusts you into the spiritual Now where the actual moment itself teaches you *everything you need to know* about how to proceed. Moving away from the mental how into the spiritual Now places you under the guiding influences of an intelligence that never fears the unknown because its very nature is understanding. To your grateful astonishment this New Intelligence does for you what you were certain you could not do for yourself. It solves the dilemma; it finds the Way. All you need to do is follow."

It doesn't matter how reluctantly you take your first step into the spiritual Now. What does matter is that you take the action. If you will do your part, the Truth will take care of the rest. This explains why the true spiritual life is said to be pathless. When it comes to leaving the mental world behind, there is no path outside of your next step ... and your next ... and your next. So what are we waiting for? The clearer we can make for ourselves the difference between the mental how and the spiritual Now the easier it becomes to depart from the one which is to enter the other. Keeping in mind what we have just learned, you may want to give the following ideas some special attention.

1. Living from the mental how:

   We often fear what we can't understand.

   Living in the spiritual Now:

   We understand that fear is a mental mistake.

2. Living from the mental how:

   We seek answers for tormenting questions.

   Living in the spiritual Now:

   We understand that there is no intelligence in torment so we simply drop those questions.

3. Living from the mental how:

   We look to the past to help guide us to a secure future

Living in the spiritual Now:

There is freedom from the past and no thought for tomorrow because we are living fully in a painless present.

4. Living from the mental how:

We are reluctant to admit when we are wrong.

Living in the spiritual Now:

We are free from the punishing need to pretend that we are always right.

5. Living from the mental how:

We spend valuable time looking back in regret over past events.

Living in the spiritual Now:

The past exists only for practical purposes and never as a source of pain or problems.

You may want to make your own list as I've done. By contrasting these two inner-conditions it will become increasingly clear to you which of these two worlds you really want to live in.

A Special Summary to Help Shatter Self-Limitation

1.

Nothing stands between you and permanent happiness.

2.

Don't ask "how," let Now show you.

3.

The spiritual Now is an unthinkable action.

4.

When traveling the inner roads, your arrival in the New

World outside of yourself is your departure from the old one.

5.

The clearer it becomes that you can't help yourself escape yourself, the freer you find yourself.

6.

You can arrive outside of yourself as quickly as you are willing to be taken there.

7.

The only path to self-success is your next step.

8.

To speed up your journey shorten the distance between the mental how and the spiritual Now.

9.

No one else can help you get outside of yourself, but you must let everyone show you the need to do so.

10.

Real success is not measured by what you are driven to achieve but by what you can quietly understand.

Detect and Reject Psychic Intruders

Imagine for a moment that you are seated in a coffee shop or a comfortable waiting area of some kind. Knowing that your higher self-education must include the quiet study of others, you spend your time profitably by discreetly observing the faces of those who are sitting all around you. Just to your left you watch the eyes of a middle-aged businessman move rapidly from side to side as if looking for something; but you know he's not seeing anything. He is under a barrage of blinding thoughts that are pressing him to resolve a problem. On your right, the lips of that attractive woman are pulled back into two thin lines. Her heart is aching over a recent rejection that keeps replaying itself in her mind. And straight ahead of you, a gray-templed gentleman is seated with his head bent over as though his thoughts are a weight he can no longer carry. Impending financial fears are pushing him down.

As you sit there quietly observing yourself and each of these others, you can see what perhaps no one else in the room has eyes to see. You know that these people have unknowingly allowed dark intruders into their psychic systems. Their inner-home, where they really live, has been temporarily invaded and taken over by negative thoughts and feelings whose sole intention is to possess and punish whoever unknowingly invites them in as guests.

Mistaking inner-intruders for welcome guests is not nearly as uncommon as you may think. Let's look at an everyday experience which each of us knows firsthand. One minute you're walking along without a care in the world and the next minute you feel as though you're carrying the entire world on your back! What has happened? Ancient history can help us to understand our own story by studying the epic tale of the Trojan Horse.

In order to deceptively enter the great fortress of their enemy which they had been unable to take by force, the Greek army built a huge, hollow wooden horse within which they hid their best soldiers. They then placed this attractive statue outside the fortress gate hoping that their enemies would think of it as a gift or a peace offering.

Not long after this, the wooden horse was accepted and taken within the fortress walls. Later that night, while everyone in the fortress slept, the hinged belly of the great horse opened and out poured the Greek soldiers who quickly defeated their unsuspecting hosts.

This amazing story can help us begin to understand how marauding thoughts and feelings get into our Inner-Home. They are unknowingly invited in whenever we can't recognize the difference between inner-friend and inner-foe. The following story illustrates how we can learn to detect and reject these psychic intruders. But, before we begin, we must first set the stage for this important Truth Tale.

Once upon a time in a world of true kings, there were certain entitled noblemen whose great land holdings were so vast that to travel by horse or carriage from one part of their estate to another could sometimes take a week or more. In order to make this journey more comfortable, which was always made by the royal family at least once a year at season's change, there were large royal roadhouses established along the way.

These well-appointed quarters also served to provide a comfortable overnight resting place for the many guests and dignitaries who would visit these noble families on a regular basis. Each royal roadhouse was well staffed all year around with a wide assortment of cooks, guards, servants and forestry men. Their sole job was to see to it that each and every one of the nobleman's visitors-in-transit was treated as a royal guest.

In charge of this staff was a chief steward who made certain that the royal roadhouse was always standing at the ready. His was the knowledge and guidance that kept everyone and everything running smoothly. And now, on with the story.

The Return of the Absent Nobleman

The nobleman and his entourage arrived at the royal roadhouse shortly after nightfall. They were on their way to the summer estate after spending the whole year traveling abroad. Everyone was glad to see the brightly lit windows and smoke bellowing chimney for they knew that this roadhouse marked the halfway point to their journey. Soon they would put their travels behind them and enjoy the rest and relaxation that comes with the quiet comfort of being in familiar surroundings.

But something was definitely wrong. Coming from inside the house the nobleman could hear loud shouting along with crashing sounds and cursing. Even as he stepped down from his carriage, the front door to the house burst open and out clattered a horse carrying a common, drunken highwayman who galloped away into the darkness. The nobleman was stunned. A moment later, to his great relief, another man appeared in the smoky door wearing the uniform of his chief steward of the house. But the nobleman's relief quickly turned into further concern because this man standing in the doorway was not the chief steward who had loyally served his family all these past years. To make matters worse, it seemed from the way this steward was responding to their arrival, that he didn't even recognize the nobleman as his employer and the royal owner of this house along the way.

After a few moments of confusion and stern correction, the steward learned just who had rolled up to the house — and soon servants were running around everywhere trying to carry out their assigned duties.

On the way into the house from the courtyard, the nobleman learned that during his family's lengthy absence from the estate, his trusted old chief steward had passed on leaving his position vacant. With no one around to appoint a new steward, all of the forestry men decided that they would share the steward's responsibilities — each taking a turn at it every other week.

As they continued to walk toward the house, the nobleman then asked who was the drunken rider and what was he doing in the house in the first place! The stand-in steward looked surprised and answered, "He was a guest of the house."

"And who invited him to stay?" replied the nobleman.

The steward looked deeply confused. "You mean, you didn't?"

Sensing a problem but not sure of its nature, the nobleman said, "Absolutely not. Where on earth would you even get such an idea?"

"Oh brother," said the steward as he reached to open the front door. "You're about to see why I thought so. There are at least twenty guests here just like that man who you saw ride out on that horse — and all of them told me they were special guests of yours. How was I to know?"

That statement had barely cleared the lips of the stand-in steward when the nobleman walked into his front parlor. He couldn't believe his eyes. Everything was in shambles. There was trash everywhere, food all over the floor, and many of his valuable possessions were either broken or altogether missing. In front of him boldly sat half a dozen highwaymen, soldiers of fortune and vagrants drinking his best brandy. A few of them were even wearing his clothes, taken from his closets. Upstairs he could hear and see a dozen more ruffians laughing and running in and out of the luxurious staterooms held for the visits of his real guests. Enough was enough. The roadhouse royal guards were summoned and within the hour the house was entirely cleared. By morning everything was as it should have been upon the nobleman's arrival. All of the uninvited bums and their guests had been cast out. The royal roadhouse was once again clean and quiet.

Being a wise and kind man, the nobleman understood that none of the stand-in stewards could as yet understand what was expected of them — so no one was punished for the damages caused by their missteps. Instead, he selected one man for the permanent position of chief steward and assigned to him a deputy who would learn the job as well. And before he left that afternoon for his summer dwelling, he called the new chief steward and his deputy to him. In their hands he placed a neatly prepared sheet of Royal Instructions that he told them must be followed precisely whenever he was away. On it was written a list of special guidelines to help them determine in the future who were the nobleman's real guests and who were the intruders only pretending to have a royal invitation. Here's how the nobleman's guest checklist read:

How To Determine Invited Guests from Unwanted Intruders

Invited guests always:

1. Announce their arrival.
2. Know their own place.
3. Act pleasant and polite.
4. Help when and where they can.
5. Keep calm.
6. Consider others.
7. Remain gracious.
8. Leave quietly.
9. Leave you feeling pleased about their presence.

Unwanted intruders always:

1. Disguise their arrival using either stealth or brashness.
2. Think they should have more than whatever is offered.
3. Create a disturbance of some kind.
4. Take self-advantage of every situation.
5. Have an uncomfortable edge about them.
6. Insist that everyone serve their wants.
7. Constantly complain that nothing is right.
8. Steal in one way or another.
9. Make you realize you are better off alone.

From that day on, the chief steward and his deputy carefully followed the nobleman's Royal Guidelines and never again did any unwanted uninvited intruder ever step within the noble walls of the royal roadhouse. They all lived happily ever after.

Without too much effort on our part, we should be able to see many, many parallels in this nobleman's story and the story of our own inner-lives. We, too, have been absent — from ourselves — from our real Inner House that was given to us to watch over by the King of Kings. In this absence of true Self-Awareness, our royal Inner-Home has slowly turned into a kind of psychic way station where all manner of negative thoughts and feelings can move in and stay as long as they please. Just like the stand-in stewards who didn't know better, we have been welcoming psychic intruders along with the real guests for so long that we have almost forgotten how to tell them apart.

Now comes the happy part of the story — of what can be your story — where the nobleman comes back home. The Truth, these Kingly Principles, say that no mental or emotional pain is authorized to dwell within you. If there is suffering in your heart, it is only because you have mistaken an unwanted intruder for a guest. Your ability to discern their difference — which you can start to do right now — is a special kind of royal entitlement giving you all the power you need to keep your Inner-Home safe from rude and thieving psychic intruders. Go back and review the nobleman's Royal Guidelines several times. Let their healthy influences awaken a new chief steward in you who will eventually see to it that your Inner-Home is truly a noble place that will remain that way forever.

Experience the Miracle of Self-Completion

I don't know if you have noticed this fairly recent change, but years ago when you went on a ride at an amusement park, it used to be that you would always get into the car just as the passengers who had already been on the ride were getting out. The newest attractions being developed today keep the end of the ride and the exiting riders some distance from its beginning so that the cars always arrive empty at the starting gate. This design is not by accident. The creators of today's rides know something about human psychology. They understand that you, the ticket buyer, are there for the thrills. But they also know that in order to bring you this kind of excitement they must somehow create the illusion that you are *really* going somewhere. So these masters of amusement do everything practically possible to hide from you the fact that the ride you're about to go on begins and ends in the same place. However, there is only so much that can be done, and the fact remains that no matter how cleverly designed — a ride is still a ride. It takes you only on a flight of fantasy and then returns you right back to where you began.

All of us have had the experience of being burned out after a day at one of these parks when the only ride we're looking forward to is the one that takes us away from the park and back to our home. These feelings are natural at the end of a big day. We just don't want any more up and down, round and round. We're tired and, to coin a phrase, the thrill is gone. We gladly accept the end of our sensational day because soon we'll be in the quiet safety of our own home where we can be fairly certain that nothing will jump out at us.

Now let's use our new knowledge of theme park rides and riders to give us a special glimpse into our own invisible inner-world of whirling thoughts and feeling. In this secret world, there are wild rides as well; rides that deliver lots of thrills and chills but which, just like those at the theme parks, take us nowhere. Most men and women unknowingly spend their entire lives getting on and off these inner-rides — living from moment to moment on a kind of emotional ferris wheel going up and up and up with each new hope or dream or answer — only to come down again and again each time they realize they were riding once more on the wrong solution. The business or marriage fails. The health fades. Or a trusted friend suddenly does an unexpected turnaround. Even feeling abandoned by life is a kind of solitary inner-ride where we rock back and forth between feelings of expectation and betrayal. The real tragedy in all of this is that after years and years of living from these rocky, up and down emotions, we eventually come to feel and believe that these kinds of churning internal sensations are Life itself. They are not. In fact, just the opposite is true.

Let the following questions and answers shed some welcome light on these important ideas.

Question: If I read you right, you're telling me that up and down feelings aren't Real Life. But isn't that why we're alive — to feel all of these amazing sensations? What else is there?

Answer: Your question takes us right to the heart of one of our greatest misunderstandings about ourselves and our real inner-potential. The up and down/down and up movement of our emotional life is not Life itself anymore than waves are all there is to an ocean. One of the ways the ocean expresses itself is by its surface movement — but what is a wave compared to the ocean's vast and unfathomable depths? So, do you see? There is a much broader way to experience this life if we would only be willing to do the necessary self-exploration.

Question: I have often thought about these things myself and so I sense the truth of what you are saying. But sensing is one thing and understanding it is another. What practical steps can I take to arrive at this realization of a greater, more complete life?

Answer: You can start by giving yourself permission to be just as dissatisfied as you really are with your present life.

Question: Why would anyone want to do that?

Answer: The clearer it becomes to you that you aren't really satisfied with the kind of life you have been giving to yourself, the sooner you will welcome the possibility of an altogether different kind of life that isn't self-generated.

Question: Please go on — is there such a life?

Answer: Prior to these Higher Studies we had always assumed that the cause of our dissatisfaction lay in how Life had treated us. Now we are learning that our feelings of unhappiness and incompleteness aren't born out of how Life has treated us but rather by what we have been calling Life. Anger, disappointment, frustration or any of their skyrocketing opposites are only sensations. This is a very important point.

Calling our up and down feelings Real Life doesn't make them so any more than calling a kitchen blender an airplane makes it capable of flight just because it hums and vibrates! Like a theme park ride, these habitual thoughts and feelings only appear to take you somewhere. In reality they are a ticket to nowhere — except right back to the need to ride again. As you become increasingly dissatisfied with where this kind of life has taken you, with what it has given you, you naturally begin to lose interest in it existence. This is a highly healthy act.

Question: Why? What does this accomplish?

Answer: Since you are no longer automatically identifying with this limited world of up and down sensations, you start to become aware of a totally new kind of inner-world. Dimly, but definitely, you can feel this calm and ever expansive Higher Life calling to you. Go. Boldly leave your self-generated self behind.

Question: What happens next? Who will I be without all of my usual feelings?

Answer: You will be that rare someone who experiences a real miracle. As you walk away from your own self-generated inner-life, you begin to discover that all of the stimulating sensations you thought were giving you life were actually separating you from it. To your grateful astonishment you realize that self-stimulation pales next to being self-completed — which is what you were looking for in the first place. Now you understand that real life is real satisfaction because as you leave the self-generated self behind, you step into the Real World where everything is already complete — including you.

The Way Out Is Safe

Picture a small wagon train winding its way across the high desert. Each of the dozen or so wagons carries a family of Easterners bound for a new life in one of the recently opened great western states. They roll slowly forward pushing against the rocks, sand and the heat. One horizon melts into another.

Then, early one evening, just after making camp, the wagon master calls his head scout over to his campfire. In subdued tones he tells the scout that he saw definite signs of Indians just before the last river crossing — and since the upcoming mountain pass is the perfect place for an ambush — he tells the scout to ride hard ahead, go through the pass, and return by daybreak with a full report. Everyone's safety, the scout is told, depends on him.

The scout listens intently to his instructions and in an instant, has understood their touchy situation. Grabbing some salt beef, biscuits, a full canteen and his Winchester rifle, he jumps onto his horse. Before the wagon master can even say goodbye he is gone — headed off into the darkness toward the distant narrow mountain pass. A coyote yells at the moonless sky. "It will be a long night," the wagon master thinks to himself. He starts a fresh pot of coffee.

Thirty minutes later a movement just outside the light of his campfire steals his attention. As he looks up from the warmth of his steaming mug, he is startled to see the head scout standing there looking back at him. Something terrible must have happened. The wagon master breaks the desert silence with a rushing, hushed question: "What are you doing back here so soon? I thought you were headed out to the pass to make sure things were safe for tomorrow's crossing."

After a long, strangely awkward pause, the head scout replies, "I was on my way when I realized there might be a problem."

"And just what might that be?" asked the wagon master.

Straining to keep his voice under control but loud enough to more than get his pressured point across, the head scout blurts out, "What if there really are Indians out there!"

This humorous little story contains an important point. To reveal its message, let's paraphrase what the head scout was really saying to the wagon master. It would go something like, "Are you kidding with that assignment? A fellow could get hurt out there ... Maybe even ride right into the wrong end of an arrow? I believe I've just lost interest in scouting — find yourself another man!"

Who can't relate to such a sudden change of heart? In those days long gone when brave men and women fought to reach new lands and win new lives, there were many more dangers than assurances along the way. History teaches us that untold numbers fell into harm's way trying to cross over from their old world and way of life into the unknown new world so rich with promise.

We're taking the time to go over this story because during our journey to a higher self, there will be those times when we are called upon to venture into dark, difficult and unknown inner-territories. Each of the wagon train characters we met in our brief visit has his place within us. For instance, the wagon master represents your own higher intuition which senses that for your continued, safe inner-progress, you must go ahead and pass through a certain resistance or reluctance that you have been avoiding. Maybe it's time you stopped running from a certain person or uncomfortable situation. Or perhaps you've been postponing a task or situation that must be done or finally resolved. You fill in the blanks. The point here is that, in your inner-travels, the way out is always through — never over or around.

As we proceed with this lesson you'll see why this is always true.

The head scout represents the part of you that is capable of acting upon higher impressions that come down from the inner-wagon master, your Higher Intuition. His task is to then try and collect the rest of you — the wagon train — which is made up of both willing travelers and teams of stubborn mules; and to help guide you to where the wagon master knows there is a new world. But, as we have seen in our story, even a head scout can have his fears and doubts. How well we all know this to be true. Again, our own inner-lives are a constant witness to the fact that knowing what we need to do and actually doing it are often two totally different things — especially when it comes to taking a step or two off the well-worn path.

Let's take a look at a few examples where the inner-wagon master says, "Ride ahead and see," and our response is, "It's too dangerous," or "I don't think I'm up to it."

You know or at least suspect that:

1. *You must stop fawning before that pushy person.*
2. *You must refuse to fall into self-pity.*
3. *You must dare to live without the approval of others.*
4. *You must place ruthless self-honesty before pleasing self-flattery.*
5. *You must boldly take another step away from yourself.*

Now please pay extra close attention. Just go ahead and *take that step* — whatever it may be. Just go ahead. You know what it is. The Truth itself promises that nothing bad will happen to you. Walk through it. That difficulty, blockage, or cruel relationship seems to be outside of you and so you fear some kind of outer repercussion, some punishment from it, if you try to break free of its influence. The truth is that each of life's terrifying mountain passes, filled with all of its unknown hostiles, is an inner affair — and on the inner-journey cannot hurt. It's true. The way out is safe. You are protected in a way that you can't think about. In fact, you mustn't think at all about the "dangers" of walking away from yourself. Instead, you must see the endangered "you" that your thinking creates! More than anything else, this higher insight quickens your step because now you know that the real danger lies not with the unexpected but with remaining where you are in your present life-level.

Assurances for Travelers on the Way

The ancient Vedic scriptures containing the inspired writings of the Bhagavad-Gita, the holy bible of the East, tells of a conversation between Lord Krishna and Arjuna. Arjuna aspires to the Higher Life but before he can attain his True Self he must face an impending conflict with many difficult trials. In one very moving section of their dialogue, Krishna, who has temporarily taken on human form in order to help Arjuna, tells him not to be afraid of the upcoming hardships he must endure. To help him take the right courage, he says that, "Neither slings nor arrows," or any other earthly weapon can bring harm to Arjuna's true self. Krishna gives him further assurance when he adds, "No heart that holds one right desire can tread the road of loss." In the end, Arjuna takes the Truth's instructions. He persists and ultimately prevails.

We, too, must persist with our walk away from ourselves. Nothing real stands between us and the life we've dreamed of. Let these assurances for Travelers on the Way put the wind at your back.

"When the heart weeps for what it has lost, the spirit laughs for what it has found."

— *Sufism*

"Yea, though I walk through the valley of the shadow of death, I shall fear no evil for Thou art with me."

— *Old Testament*

"Higher, deeper, innermost, abides Another Life."

— *Bhagavad-Gita*

"The Truth is the end and aim of all existence, and the worlds originate so that the Truth may come and dwell therein. Those who fail to aspire for the Truth have missed the purpose of life. Blessed is he who rests in the Truth."

— *Buddhism*

"God hath not given us the Spirit of fear; but of power, and of love, and of a sound mind."

— New Testament

CHAPTER 8

Dare to Let Go and Live as You Please

Let's look to the brilliant scientist, inventor and successful corporate businessman Charles Franklin Kettering for some very special guidance. His farsighted understanding led him to many outstanding patents and achievements in the early years of the automobile industry. As you are about to see, we can all benefit from Mr. Kettering's unique insight into the secret of solving problems. He believed that a problem was willing to be solved, provided the solution-seeker remembered who was boss, by which Mr. Kettering meant the *problem,* not the seeker. He used to say to his coworkers that the only difference between a problem and a solution is that people *understand* the solution. Solutions only involve a *change in perception*, since the solution must have existed all along—right there *within the problem*. The task, he used to say, was not to master the problem but to make it give birth to its solution.

This higher kind of thinking can be applied to every difficult situation. At its root is the powerful idea that illumination is superior to domination. Now, ask yourself which you would rather do: Temporarily subdue a painful personal problem and then live with the knowledge that you will have to fight with it again one day, or let go of that unhappy condition altogether by seeing through it to its *actual* cause? There is really no choice. And that's why, each time we are faced with a personal problem, we must choose in favor of our True Self by voluntarily suspending our usual solution-seeking reactions. Again, the key is to let the problem reveal *its* real nature to you. Only a look at the real problem can reveal the *real* solution. To make this dynamic principle a little clearer, let's look at a simple illustration.

Imagine a man in his home who suddenly starts feeling uncomfortably cold. He puts on a heavy coat, but it doesn't help warm him. His feet are freezing. He then turns up the home heating, but he still can't shake the persistent chill. He's bewildered. He starts worrying that he may be coming down with something, so he takes some medication and considers calling the doctor. And then, quite by accident, he notices that one of the curtains drawn across his back-porch French doors seems to be gently waving. He walks over to the doors and pulls back the curtain. All at once his fears of getting sick vanish. Now everything is so obvious. The source of the big chill was the open French doors, which allowed the wintery cold air to roll across his floor. All he has to do to get warm and to stay that way is shut the open door.

One of the main lessons to be taken from this simple story for self-study is that our real problems, however they may appear at first, are almost never what we initially think them to be. Nowhere is this more true than when it comes to our unsuccessful attempts at living life as we please. Following are four paragraphs specially designed to help us see how the new and true solution for self-independence arises out of revealing the real inner problem.

We think *the problem is—*

It's hard to be our own person and live freely as we please when there are certain people or difficult circumstances always demanding our compromise.

Our immediate usual solution *is*—

Assert ourselves as far as is reasonable after weighing each situation, but never go beyond our ability to protect what we already call our own.

When necessary, avoid any situation there is no hope of changing.

The unhappy results *are*—

A life of constant conflict, because most of our time is spent comparing what we stand to gain against what we might lose should we dare to make a stand for ourselves.

However, the real problem *is*—

Something within our own psychic system is silently but surely spreading the spoken and emotional message that we should just go ahead and yield to superior forces; that we may as well give up because the chances against winning a life that is happily our own are just too great.

Pause now for a moment and reflect on just how often and persistently you have heard and felt this sad sentiment right within you. To better understand the purpose of these inner voices of gloom and inescapable defeat we need to study the fascinating war techniques of Genghis Khan.

Your Ultimate Victory Over Harmful Inner Voices

It is a little-known fact that Genghis Khan defeated many of his enemies from *within* their own rank-and-file using psychological warfare. Some of his victories even took place without a fight. Here's how he subdued his enemies without their knowing it. Khan would send specially trained agents well in advance of his own approaching army, and these spies, acting as common peasants, would infiltrate the camp of his enemy. Once they were fully accepted by Khan's enemies, they would then start spreading frightening stories about the vast size, strength and invincibility of Khan's forces. Since these stories seem to be coming from the army's own people— who had no apparent reason to lie— they were taken as the truth. Therefore, there was no choice for Khan's rivals but to surrender in the face of such impossible odds.

This historic information illustrates exactly what has happened inwardly to you and me. Try and see it. We too have been invaded without knowing it. And, just like Khan's unsuspecting rivals, we have mistakenly embraced the enemy as our own. In this instance we are deceived by our own false nature, which is always telling us to play it safe and to compromise whatever is necessary to insure our psychological security. We wrongly believe that this warning, arising from within us, is there to protect us from the daily attacks of an insensitive world. The truth is, these alarming inner-warnings, which always bear some kind of ill-tiding, *are the only attack there is*. Our problem, up until now, has been that we haven't been able to see the whole picture. In our minds, just as it was cleverly planted into the minds of Khan's enemies, the only sensible thing to do when faced with overwhelming challenges is to negotiate the best terms we can get for ourselves and learn to live with the rest. We are learning that what appears to be legions of impossible difficulties are actually nothing but an army of dark imaginings— and that these troubled thoughts and feelings of ours are the only forces that keep us from having and enjoying life on our own terms.

"I can understand what you have been saying and I think I even recognize a few of my own inner invaders— like worrying over what someone will think about me if I go ahead and do what's right; or timid thoughts that tell me I am better off taking the easy way than to challenge myself. But I must be missing something. How do you move from just recognizing these unwelcome inner intruders to actually removing them from your psychic system?"

"Your willingness to investigate and reveal the inner operations of the false self will lead you to an amazing and inescapable conclusion. The clearer it becomes to you that your real and only problem is bad inner company, the sooner you'll be moved to forsake it and start living alone inwardly."

"Can that really be done?"

"Yes. In the world of people and places, we must learn about and take part in many kinds of relationships. This is right and good and a natural necessity filled with many natural comforts. But unlike living in the outer world, where being with others cannot be avoided, in the inner world just the opposite is true. *Inwardly there is nothing that can stop us from being alone,* and *that* is our ultimate victory over harmful voices and scary feelings. They must have our ear or they have no one to talk to."

Practice living alone inwardly and one day the word "alone" won't frighten you anymore, because there will be no darkness left within your psychic system talking to you about how lonely you feel. On that glad day you will have won your own free life. You will live as you please every day. And from the abundance of your new independence will come a lasting confidence and cheer, for now you know you need answer *only* to yourself.

Clear This Obstacle and Climb to True Independence

Real self-independence is the fruit of an awakened inner life. And just as fruit on a tree must develop into fullness following a certain order of natural events, so too is there a natural order of self-realizations that lead up to winning your own life and living it as you please.

Every step along the way to this higher independent life is both the challenge and the reward. The challenge is always in how dark and uncertain the next step appears to be; and the reward, *after* you take the step, is the sweet and relief-filled discovery that who you really are cannot fall! In this way, step by step, a man or a woman walks into the fullness of their own independent, true nature.

However, as with any climb to a loftier view, there are always those spots that are more difficult than others to negotiate. The more light we can shed on these psychological outcrops that obscure our vision, the smoother our upward journey will be. Remember, the Truth will never lead you to an impasse. If it ever seems that way, it is only because you are needlessly trying to take something along with you that can't be part of the Higher Life which awaits you just ahead. So let go. You will rise to the next step effortlessly.

One of the major obstacles in the climb to self-independence, where many students falter and so fail to take the next important step upward, is in their reluctance to see that the actual human condition is far worse off than they ever imagined. *You* must be different. As you are about to see, only your unwavering insight into the low life-level of society and its economic and religious leaders can bring into play the Higher Forces necessary to transform you into a truly independent person. So you must never hesitate to see through people, nor should you ever feel guilty for what your Higher Vision reveals to you about them. This guilty feeling, as if you've done something bad by seeing badness in others, is a trick of the false self. It needs to keep you believing in others so that later on you can feel stressed and betrayed when they fail to live up to your expectations. In his stunningly powerful pocketbook, *50 Ways to See Through People*, Vernon Howard explains exactly why we must never feel bad about seeing badness.

> "Some students of human nature are reluctant about exposing falseness and weakness in others. They think

> they should not see so much badness. The opposite is right. You should and must know all about hurtful human behavior, for only exposure of the wrong can invite the right. The real peril is to *not* see things as they are, for delusion is dangerous to the deluded. Believing that a shark is a dolphin is both foolish and unnecessary. When a wise man sees a shark he knows it is a shark. Since when is it wrong to see right?"[1]

So it is both wise and profitable to collect facts about the weakness of human nature. Indeed, if our search for true independence is to have a happy ending, we must learn not only to welcome these temporarily shocking insights but we must gather ourselves up and ask to see more. The Truth will oblige. Here are three friendly facts to help us let go and grow more spiritually independent.

Fact 1: You can only depend on others for as long as it pays them to tolerate your dependence.

Fact 2: No matter how it may appear on the surface of human events, *self-interest* governs individuals.

Fact 3: Even the typical display of human kindness or benevolence comes not from that person's compassionate nature, but from his unconscious desire to enrich himself with the intoxicating feelings of being a good person. Forget to thank him or acknowledge his generosity and watch how quickly his goodness turns into repressed resentment or outward indignation.

These higher facts are not negative. What is negative is to hide from ourselves that we have been betrayed by others. The evidence is overwhelming.

Depending on others for a sense of independent psychological well-being is an accident waiting to happen. You

[1] *Vernon Howard, 50 Ways to See Thru People, (New Life, 1981)*

do not have to live with this kind of fear for one more moment. If you will give yourself permission to see the whole truth about human nature and its affairs, the Truth will show you something about yourself that will lift you high above any of your present painful concerns. So don't be afraid to come to the temporarily disturbing but wonderful understanding that *there is no one for you to count on* — because there isn't — at least not where you have been looking. This gradual realization of your true and present position in life is actually a step up. It only feels like a step down. And the only reason it feels like this is because, unknown to yourself, you have been living with the self-limiting belief that one day someone would give you what you haven't been able to give to yourself— true independence. Well, the wait is over and so is the fear.

Let me show you a secret and miraculous part of yourself that only reveals itself when you are willing to stand in the light of the truth about yourself and others. You are on the verge of discovering what few men and women ever come to realize; your secret power for self-independence. This wise and uncompromised inner strength is patiently waiting for you to fulfill the laws that govern its entrance into your life.

The following short story about a fledgling eaglet will help illustrate just how these beautiful laws might work in nature. The surprise ending contains a great mystery. Let it reveal to you something wondrous and unthinkable about yourself. Then, gather all the facts in this chapter section and make it your aim to settle for nothing less than your own surprise happy ending.

Start Soaring Above Yourself

The young eaglet had stood on the stick-woven edge of his nest before. He wasn't exactly sure why he liked having his face to the wind, but standing there looking down at the rocky cliffs, woods and streams below always sent an indescribable feeling coursing through his body. He just liked it there; king of the world beneath him. And life was good. His parents brought him food every day and rains did the housecleaning. He had always felt fortunate beyond others to be able to live in such a lofty fashion.

But today was different. Something was definitely wrong. He could feel it, and he was worried. It wasn't just that he was all alone either. In fact, he had been all by himself now for a few days. Sure, he was hungry and maybe even a little lonely, but the big thing on his mind at the moment was the fact that something he had never seen before was inching its way across the craggy outcrop headed straight for his nest. Instinctively, he knew that whatever this four-legged creature was, it wasn't showing it's large teeth to him as a greeting. He decided to warn off the intruder and mustered his best warning shrill. No good. If anything, his warning only excited his stalker. Now it was less than a few feet away.

The young eaglet hopped to the other side of his branched aerie with the idea of putting some unsure footing between him and his pursuer. This would have probably worked except for the fact that right there, waiting for him on the opposite facing rock outcrop, not three feet from his new position was another fanged creature just like the one he had momentarily escaped. And this one wanted him too! There weren't too many choices left now. The young eaglet moved out to the very center edge of the nest. Questions raced through his mind. Where were Mom and Dad? Was this supposed to be happening? Who or what could help him now? Things looked very bleak. He turned and faced the great openness that spread out beneath him. There were no choices left. Better to leap and risk the fall than to face the creatures who were now only inches away. "What a way to go," he thought to himself. And with that, his little heart pounding, he closed his eyes and jumped into the great nothingness. There was just no other way.

He could have never dreamed what happened next. As the rocky ground below him started racing up to meet him, something from deep within him issued an order and the young eaglet spread open his arms to catch himself. But instead of catching the unforgiving rocks, his arms caught the wind. Up and away he soared from what he had thought was certain doom. In that moment, he had found his wings. Never again would he be alone or afraid. The sky was now his true home.

The most important point to ponder in this Truth Tale is that you too have wings; a very special and secret part of yourself that you don't as yet know belong to you. Living under the defeatist directions of the false self, we wrongly assume that the only way to reach real independence, real safety, is to look to someone else to take us there. It isn't in another's power to do for you what you must do for yourself. It never has been. Whenever one tries to fly for two, a crash always occurs. Stop looking for what you hope to see in others and start seeing what you need to see. The clearer your vision becomes the sooner you will be forced out of the nest and into the air where you belong. Your true nature is already fully independent and flying freely. Let go.

Higher Hints for Taking Charge of Yourself

1

Before you turn to another person for help, honestly see if he has ever really *helped himself. Look for his wings, not at his words.*

2

When you understand that no one really knows who they are, you will stop looking to them to tell you who you *are.*

3

Neither the approval nor the disapproval of any individual or group makes any real difference in the quality of your life.

4

People always want you to be who they *want you to be in order to please them. Be yourself and please yourself.*

5

Why do you want the approval of those who don't even approve of themselves?

6

When you know where you are going, you are free from any concern over where anyone else is going.

7

If you don't leap, you'll never know what it's like to fly.

8

In daily contact with others, if you are not aware of the other person's weakness, he is probably aware of yours.

9

Ninety-nine people can approve you, but if the one-hundredth scowls, your day is ruined.

10

If you are headed for the mountain top, why do you care what the people in the valley are doing?

Let Go of These Secret Life-Draining Demands

If a man with a gun walks up to you and demands your money, you give him your wallet. You don't ask him why or argue. You resign yourself to cooperate with the bandit's cruel demand because there is no other reasonable option. Simply stated, your fear of great bodily harm outweighs your love of money and so you are compelled to obey his demand.

I am making this point about demands because wherever you find someone *demanding* something you must also find someone else who is being forced or coerced to cooperate. This is important to understand if we want to learn how to answer the demands of this world. No one *demands* something from someone that would be freely given to him if he didn't demand it. This should be obvious to us. For instance, you would never demand that someone love you. Either love is given to you freely or it is not love. The point being made here is that anywhere or anytime you have relationships that place demands on you — of any kind — you are in the midst of a "play or pay the consequences" situation.

In our imaginary scenario involving the gun-wielding robber, the consequences of our failure to obey his demands are obvious. But now let's consider the other countless demands that are made on us every day; demands that rob us not only of our money but of our ability to laugh and be happy — insidious demands that steal our peace of mind. Let's bring some of these life-draining demands out into the open.

List Number One

The world demands that we should:

1. Give our undivided support to political pressure groups.
2. Conform to social mandates.
3. Excuse rude behavior.
4. Keep a nervous eye on world events.
5. Give our smiling approval to everyone.
6. Have unquestioning loyalty for family members.
7. Look at life as a race to win.
8. Compromise whatever is necessary to succeed.
9. Involve ourselves in other people's lives.
10. Respect bums.

Incredibly, this short list of worldly demands reveals only a tiny fraction of the aggravated assault we are forced to face each and every day. But the truth is these common worldly offenses are nothing compared to the everyday punishing demands we place on ourselves! Just look at the next list.

List Number Two

We demand of ourselves that we should:

1. Be in complete control of everything around us.
2. Be an inspiration to all we meet.
3. Be ruthless in our honesty about others.
4. Be tireless in our efforts to succeed.
5. Be infallible in the eyes of others.
6. Be a source of strength for the less fortunate.
7. Be rich, famous and eternally slim.
8. Be wise beyond doubt in all matters.
9. Be an important person.
10. Be all things to all people!

Interestingly enough, it is these very self-generated demands that ultimately give rise to the exhausting list of worldly demands. This is yet another example of how the inner determines the outer. As an interesting inner exercise, look and see how number 9 of list one can be traced back to number 10 of list two; or how number 2 of list one is born out of number 7 in list two. These connections are obvious. Some others are more subtle. You may want to draw some parallels of your own between the two lists or, for an even better exercise in self-study, make up your own lists. As the hidden connection between these two seemingly different worlds grows clearer in your mind, so will your understanding about the only way to answer *all* of their demands.

Freedom to Answer the World the Way You Want

"If I'm understanding you so far, you are saying I have

been 'holding the gun' on myself. But why would anyone want to do that to himself?"

"No one *wants* to be a hold-up victim. Inner and outer crimes all take place in the darkness of ignorance long before they express themselves in the light of day. We unconsciously place these punishing demands on ourselves because each of us wants to be greater than we are."

"Well, what's wrong with wanting to be a better person?"

"Nothing at all. But trying to live up to the picture you have of yourself as being a better person *doesn't* make you better— it only makes you bitter towards every person and event that threatens this picture."

"What do you mean?"

"One example of this self-imposed bitterness occurs each time you feel resentful towards someone who isn't properly appreciative of your helpful kindness. What this resentment shows is that you really didn't want to give your help in the first place. You felt *compelled* to do so by the picture you have of yourself as being kind or helpful."

"I think you may be right. But where do these painful pictures we paint of ourselves come from? How do we wipe the canvas clean so we don't have to suffer at the hands of these self-defeating self-images anymore?"

"You diminish the strength of these destructive and demanding self-pictures by learning to see through them— which includes the full understanding of how these self-pictures come to be formed in your psyche."

"Can we really see all of this in ourselves?"

"Absolutely. One of the main reasons we paint pretty pictures of ourselves is because we unconsciously fear that somewhere within us a darkness dwells. Maybe it's a longtime hatred of someone, or a selfishness or anger that we just can't seem to drop. Fearing this darkness in ourselves, we are moved to imagine its opposite— a kind of self-designed champion or hero who is miraculously free of the failings he was created to overcome. The only problem with this self created super-self is that it's only strength seems to be its peculiar ability to make us feel bad for being so weak!"

"I know exactly what you mean. But what do we do? It can't be right to just let this inner-darkness go unchallenged."

"Let the Light fight for you. Only it can succeed in this battle. Permit it to *show* you— no matter how it may appear otherwise— that this unseen but emotionally perceived inner-darkness is just as much a self-picture as is its silly and self-flattering super-self opposite. In fact these self-pictures are constantly born out of one another, which is why there seems to be no end to them or their demands. But there *is*. Once you see that who you really are is not *any* picture you may have of yourself— good or bad— you are also freed from the unconscious and compulsive need to live up to that picture's demands. Now you are free to answer this world— and everyone in it— the way *you* want."

"Believe me, I would like to be that strong, but mustn't we give in to certain demands? I don't want to lose anything by being too rigid."

"The only thing you risk losing, if you'll embrace this new self-understanding, is the feeling that someone has a gun on you. Remember the lesson. You *always* resent what you are unconsciously compelled to do. This includes the painful act of pretending to care for others whose only idea of caring for you is to demand that you be the kind of person they can care for."

"I would like to start freeing myself *right* now. Where do I start?"

"Begin with the higher fact that you are not here on earth to live up to anyone's expectations— *including your own*. There is something much higher to *be* in this life than someone who is compelled to *do*. Your True Self knows that there is only one supreme command. And that is: *You need never answer any demand that causes you pain or that asks you to sacrifice your integrity*."

Walk Lightly Through Life

Whenever you come upon a healing idea or a rescuing truth, it is almost always a surprise that you could have missed something that was so obvious for so long. Do you know the feeling? More than anything else, a glimpse of a Timeless Truth is a lot like rounding a bend and suddenly seeing something you know you knew a long, long time ago; like discovering all over again a special place you once loved.

You can't explain it but these out-of-the-blue higher moments seem as much a trusted memory as they do a gateway to a new and exciting understanding. Our life is intended to be filled with magical moments such as these. Settling for anything less is an unseen compromise that suffers the Spirit. This is why the real successes in life are more an awakening than they are an arrival at a thrilling but temporary destination. Let the following short story stir you to remember something your true nature has never forgotten.

It seemed he had been walking for a very long time. But even more than his weary legs he was aware of his hands. They were starting to feel like they were part of the bags he was carrying.

"This is no better," he thought to himself, as he tried to shift some of the baggage's weight from one aching part of his hands to another. He wished he could put them all down, but he was in a hurry.

It was hard to believe that only a few hours had passed since he had run into that nice man selling bags alongside the road. The bag-seller had promised him that buying one of his bags would make carrying all of the other bags a lot easier. But, as he walked along, he could think of a lot of other words to describe what the addition of this new bag had done for him. "Easier" certainly wasn't one of them. And this wasn't the first bag he had been sold along the road. Not by any means.

As he looked down at his stiffening arms and hands, it seemed to him as though every bag he was carrying had been guaranteed for one thing or another. He had a bag of plans for the future; a bag that held keys to success; a bag of miscellaneous kits for repairing the past; and then there was the heaviest bag of all: The one that was supposed to keep all of his other bags safe. The truth was that he owned a bag for just about everything imaginable.

So involved was he in assessing and reassessing the value of all of his bags that he didn't even notice the stranger sitting in the shade off to the side of the road. In fact, it was the stranger's voice that made him look up from his bags. The stranger smiled.

"That's quite a load you've got there. Care to sit a while and take a break?"

The notion surprised him for some reason but it sounded like a good idea. "Thanks," he said, "I think I will." And he sat his bags down, one by one, lined up according to their size. A moment or two passed without either of them speaking, but it wasn't uncomfortable. The grass was soft and just damp enough to feel good. The only thing strange was that he noticed the stranger didn't have any bags with him at all. Not one. To the best of his recollection this was a first. All of the men and women he had met along the road carried some kind of bag. How could he survive? What kind of person was this? How did he meet the challenges of the road? His mind started racing with one silent question after another, but he knew it would be too impolite to say anything. He couldn't believe his own ears when the words jumped out of his mouth.

"I see you don't have any bags."

The stranger smiled back at the man. "No, that's right."

The man waited for further explanation but none came. Finally the silence became too heavy. "Why not?" he asked.

The stranger had heard many questions like his before from other travelers he had met along the way. Experience had long taught him that most of these questions placed before him by others— as to why he traveled so lightly— were not asked in order to hear his answer. No. Most only feigned interest. What they were really seeking was a way to tell him their view on the subject. But he sensed that this weary man across from him was different from the rest. And so he answered with the truth.

"One day, years ago, I was taking a break in a shady spot just like this one when a familiar voice spoke to me. I knew I had heard that voice at least a thousand times before and yet, right up to that moment, I had never really heard it."

The stranger seemed to look off into the past but he kept talking. "It was strange, because the voice just kept saying over and over again, 'I'm so tired, how much further do we have to go?' That's all— just, 'I'm so tired' and 'how much further?'"

"Who were you with?" the man asked.

"No one," the stranger replied and looked back at him with a deep kind of self-conscious smile. "I was all by myself. And I don't know why I should have taken notice of it just then, but that's when it happened. I realized that for as many years as I cared to remember, I had been talking to myself about how tired I was."

The stranger's answer came as an unexpected shock. He wanted to pity this empty-handed man but instead he was drawn to him and to what he was saying. His silence was the invitation for the stranger to continue talking.

"At first I tried to push my sorry realization away by thinking about another bag I had always wanted. But by this time I was even tired of those feelings. I didn't know what else to do so I just sat there. I can't really say for how long. And then it came to me." The stranger smiled again and the man thought that maybe he had missed something. But if he had, the stranger didn't pause long enough for him to ask. "It wasn't so much that I didn't feel like going anywhere as it was I had realized, while sitting there, that for all of my years on the road I had never really known where I was going. Only until that day I never knew that I didn't know because, for all of those same years on the road, I had come to believe that my search for relief was the same as having a direction in life."

"But why were you seeking relief; I mean, what from?"

"That's the crazy thing," the stranger said starting to laugh quietly to himself as if he had heard a good joke. "I was looking for relief from all the baggage I was carrying— bags that were supposed to make my walk through life an enjoyable one!"

Now they both laughed the good laugh like two old friends who were in on a private joke. The warmth of their shared understanding was still there when the man broke in. "But where are your bags now?"

"That's the whole point," replied the stranger still with a smile on his face. "Don't you see? If I didn't know where I was going then how could I possibly know what I needed to get me there?" It was his eyes that asked for a reply.

"Right," the man said before he knew it.

"So then, why on earth was I carrying all of those bags? The truth is that I couldn't come up with any good answer so I just left them right there where I had been sitting."

"Well, what happened next? Where did you go? How did your life change?"

The stranger's look stopped his flood of questions. "It took some time but gradually I began to see that it wasn't so much *my* life that was changing as it was that my *view* of life had changed. Without the burden of all of the bags I had been carrying I started seeing life as a wonderful place to *be* instead of a task to go *through*."

The man could sense the truth in the stranger's words and he wanted more explanation. "A wonderful place to be?"

"Yes." The stranger started to get up and brushed the leaves from his pants. "For one thing, I found that I was always right where I wanted to be once I stopped making myself miserable for not being where I thought I should be." He looked directly at the man. "*The truth is, you don't need to be who you think you have to be. Therefore, you don't have to carry those things through life you think you need to make you that person.*" And with that the stranger said, "See you later," and started walking away.

The man bolted to his feet, "Where are you going?"

The stranger didn't reply but he wasn't rude.

The man looked down at the long line of his heavy bags and looked back up at the light step of the stranger as he walked down the road. It only took another second for him to make up his mind. "Wait for me!"

Think of all the things you feel you need to carry through your life in order to keep your life going according to the way you *think* it should go. Weigh all of the facts you've learned. Now think how nice it would be to let go of all of that.

Keys for Living Lightly

Here are special steps you can take to find the light life that comes with letting go of yourself. Remember, it is insight into our problems that makes them reveal their secret solutions. Insight is self-light. Self-light is the key to a light-stepping self.

1. *Real life is intended to be inner-activated, not outer-directed.*

2. *Only wrongness needs to check with itself to see if it's right.*

3. *You can have a relationship with something you don't understand, but that relationship will always be on its terms.*

4. *To soar more, see more.*

5. *Stop trying to act kind and dare to be more awake — for the kindest act of all is to help another see through the hoax of unhappiness.*

6. *As long as you act as though your life depends upon anything temporal, it does.*

7. *Your secret strength knows that your secret weakness isn't yours at all.*

8. *False life is exhausting; real life is inexhaustible.*

9. *Any confidence you may have based on something outside yourself is also the basis of your self-doubt.*

10. *If you allow others to tell you where you are going, then you must also depend on them to tell you what you will* need *for your journey.*

CHAPTER 9

Contact with the Secret Self

Letting go of who you think you are and making contact with the Secret Self are actually one and the same. But what is the Secret Self? We don't have to look upon this invisible part of ourselves as anything mysterious, for it is not. In fact, this sacred nature within wants only to reveal itself and to show those with eyes to see the wonders of their own hidden heavens. This is what our self-studies over the past eight chapters have been leading us to: Making contact with the Secret Self.

Learning to let go of our own constant mental chattering prepares us for the entrance of the Secret Self. And when, at last, we would rather listen for its coming than to our own internal talking, this Sovereign Self makes its appearance. In that instant, all is changed. All is new. Heraclitus, the Greek philosopher of ancient Ephesus who rejected his own city-kingship in favor of contacting this force of true higher self-command, grasped the importance of willingly suspending the common in favor of the promise of the celestial:

"If one does not expect the unexpected, one will not

find it; for it is not reached by search or by trail."

What would our contact with this exalted secret "unexpectedness" reveal? What does this higher nature of ours know that we don't? Seekers of the Secret Self, the wise and illuminated men and women who have kept what is good and true aflame through the ages, have left us accounts of their findings. These royal records are meant to encourage and strengthen us in our own search for higher self-meaning. A brief glance at a few of these inspired instructions shows that the Secret Self not only knows all about our present unhappiness, but it is also trying to reach us and teach us that no heartache is necessary.

1. *The Secret Self knows the folly of our wisdom* and invites us to go beyond our present limited thinking into the fullness of its Knowing:
   "Happy is the man that findeth True Wisdom, and the man that getteth Understanding . . . she is more precious than rubies: And all things thou canst desire are not to be compared unto her." (Old Testament)

2. *The Secret Self knows the fear in our hopes* and promises that true fearlessness will come to anyone who dares to seek it first.
   "He who has found the bliss of the Eternal has no fear from any corner." (Upanishads)

3. *The Secret Self knows the frustration in our demands* and wisely instructs us to accept the relief and release that comes with wanting what it wants.
   "Resign yourself to the sequence of things, forgetting the changes of life, and you shall

enter into the Pure, the Divine, the One." (Taoism)

4. *The Secret Self knows the anguish of our attachments* and assures us that letting go of what we think we must have to be happy is the same as letting go of our unhappiness.
   "If we liberate our souls from our petty selves, wish no ills to others, and become clear as a crystal diamond reflecting the light of Truth, what a radiant picture will appear in us, mirroring things as they are, without the admixture of our burning desires, without the distortion of erroneous illusion, without the agitation of clinging and unrest." (Buddhism)

5. *The Secret Self knows the hollow in our hearts* and decrees that if we will place it above all other loves that it will place us above all of our emptiness.
   "A new heart also will I give you, and a new spirit will I put within you." (New Testament)

You Can Reach Whatever You Are Willing to Receive

Most men and women searching for the secret of letting go make one mistake in common. They listen to their own conclusions. This is tragic. In as many ways as possible, the Truth is trying to teach us that the limit of our present life-level is not the limit of life's possibilities. This entire book is about coming to the realization that what is possible for us to become only truly changes when we are willing to see what is impossible for us to continue being. This is the Secret of Secrets. This is the secret of letting go. And while these higher ideas may take patient self-study and considerable explanation, those who are willing to listen will receive everything they need to let go and grow. Here are a few questions that always seem to surface following a class discussion about letting go and contacting the Secret Higher Self.

Q: The Secret Self sounds wonderful but I have this sinking feeling that it may be beyond my reach.
A: Of course it is. That's just the point. But *our* reach is not the conclusion. If it were, we would all be doomed to do nothing but go round and round in the closed circle of the false self.

Q: But if we can't reach the Secret Self, then how do we make contact?
A: This is where millions of seekers of the liberated life lose their way. You do not contact the Secret Self. We cannot. The lower nature has absolutely no authority or influence over the Higher. None. The Secret Self enters only that individual's life who has prepared the way for its entrance. It comes by invitation alone.

Q: Isn't there something we can do to help prepare ourselves?
A: Oh, yes. There is no greater power for inviting this cosmic goodness into your life than your willingness to be receptive. As you will see, learning to listen *is* learning to ask for this exalted self-newness.

We can gather more valuable insight into this fascinating subject from author Vernon Howard. In his extraordinary book, *The Power of Your Supermind*, he advises:

"Individual receptivity is everything. Without it, nothing changes. With it, all things are possible for you.

"Contact with the truth brings out either the best or the worst in a man. When we hear the truth, it falls either on the true self or the false self. If it falls on the artificial

self, it will be rejected, distorted, or ignored, doing no good for the individual. But if a person has a welcoming attitude, the truth falls on his authentic self, providing understanding and relief.

"Receptivity is a matter of degree. Our task is to set out the welcoming mat more and more, enabling it to increasingly aid us. A little receptivity opens the way for more, for each rewarding experience shows us that the truth we once feared and rejected is the very happiness we want."[1]

Whenever or wherever I happen to be teaching, I always stress the importance of learning to listen. In a moment I will ask you to set this book down and to just listen for a moment. But when you do, I want you to try listening in a new way. I want you to listen with *all of you* to *all of you*. Listen as though every part of your mind and body is trying to hear something. Don't be concerned with what you are trying to hear or even what direction to listen in. That will ruin it. Just be as open and attentive as you know how. Expect the unexpected.

Here is a helpful hint that may aid you in bringing this inner exercise into focus. Do you remember ever being in bed all alone, late at night, and suddenly hearing an unexplained noise? In that instant, every fiber of your being was doing one thing: Listening! Now go ahead and practice this new kind of listening for a minute or two and then we'll resume our studies.

If we have really listened, we may have found ourselves with a vague kind of uncomfortable feeling. Don't push this feeling away. Everything depends upon our being receptive to it. It contains an important message. A personal anecdote from my own past will help us to better understand the nature of our unusual discovery in self listening.

Vernon Howard, *The Power of Your Supermind*, Prentice Hall, *1967).*

To Hear the Song of the Secret Self

Once, some years ago, I was doing some routine landscaping work, and to help pass the time I brought out a small portable radio. Having once been a composer, I enjoyed listening to the melodic lines of popular songs. It was a beautiful sunlit day, and the easy music from the radio seemed to blend right in.

As the time wore on, I began to feel a little disconcerted. Something was bothering me. But elbow-deep as I was in my work, and with so much more to do, I just discounted the feeling without even knowing that I had done so. The next thing I knew I was feeling anxious, edgy. But why? I didn't want to stop working just to acknowledge that I was getting irritable, so I threw myself back into the job. A few minutes later there was no denying it. I knew I had to come to a stop and address these unexplainable feelings.

As I stood there, aware of my surroundings once again, listening came effortlessly. And so did my surprise. The unexplained disturbance I was feeling was no longer the unexplained. Now it was clear.

The conflict I had been feeling wasn't *my* conflict at all. It was coming from the radio! So engrossed had I been in my work I never noticed that the signal from the radio station I was listening to had drifted—and where before there had been only one soothing sound—now there were two or three stations fading in and out all at once. For some time the "pleasant music" I had unconsciously been listening to was really an unearthly blend of dissimilar musics mixed in with intermittent bursts of bad news. The invisible but deep inner lesson behind this story is conclusive: If we aren't *listening* we are hearing without knowing what we are *receiving*.

In our everyday life, as witnessed by my tale of the drifting radio signal, this kind of self-unawareness leads to countless, unnecessarily uncomfortable moments. Just one example of this can be seen when we *think* that someone else may be thinking about us in a negative manner. We then react towards that person defensively, which produces the very isolation we feared. If, on the other hand, we knew that we had "received" that self-produced self-defeating thought—if we had "heard" it come in—we could have just discounted it as the unimportant nonsense that it was instead of giving our lives over to its negative influence. So we can see that our life, for the good or bad of it, is very much determined by what we receive. This new understanding of ours has implications that reach far beyond ordinary events—all the way to the stars.

The *Secret Self*, the foundation of all goodness, is forever sending out its cosmic strength and silent wisdom. Our task isn't so much to reach for this God nature as it is to allow it to reach us by receiving its healing influences. Do you see this? This important insight brings us to a pivotal point in our efforts to make contact with the Secret Self.

Before we can receive the spiritual gifts of the Secret Self into our lives, we must first remove the obstacles that have been preventing its entrance. So the first stage of being truly receptive is to notice where we are *not*. To say this in other words, higher receptivity requires us to first see where we have unconsciously permitted disruptive negative influences to occupy our minds and hearts.

I should point out that this level of self-study proves a stumbling block to many students. Indeed, it is hard to understand the seeming contradiction in why higher self-attention and real self-listening should often be attended by a kind of constant conscious discomfort. After all, the incorrect reasoning goes, if we are really doing the higher work we should be feeling the higher feelings. Yes and no is the Truth's reply, for the explanation is both simple and profound. When we are truly receptive we can "hear" the dissonance in our own psychic system. And the more we can "hear" the healthier we become, because each conscious detection of a sour inner note is the beginning of the end of it. Here is how this works.

True harmony already exists. All of us know this in our hearts, even if the confused affairs of men seem to prove otherwise. This Celestial Harmony, the Song of the Secret Self, is what in scale enables a master orchestra conductor to detect even the slightest mistuned instrument from out of a hundred that may be playing. In a similar fashion, the Secret Self can "hear" our most subtle discordant inner state. But its awareness of this negativity is *not negative*. This higher awareness is outside of the negative state, or it could not perceive it as negative. Again, the master conductor's ability to hear a bad outer note comes to him from his own perfect inner pitch.

You too can call upon a hidden and royal inner resource that knows exactly what should and shouldn't be sounding within you. Beginning right now, this moment, permit yourself to start listening to yourself more and more each day. And never mind if you start noticing strange thoughts and feelings that seem strained or sad. Your task is simply to stay receptive. Have no concerns over the nature of what you "hear." Your false nature will want you to turn these false inner notes into another sad song. Stay silent. Just let these negative thoughts and feelings remain right where they are—which is *within your awareness that they are out of place*. That is all you need to do. Your awareness of their out-of-placeness — of their disharmony — is coming to you from the Secret Self. It *knows* what you are just beginning to sense. It knows that there is no *real* place in you for any sorry sound.

The Kingdom of the Secret Self

Once upon a long time ago, a good but aging ruler of a distant country decided the time had come to teach his young son a most important lesson about the royal nature of a true king. He instinctively knew it wouldn't be too much longer before the crown prince would have to assume his monarch's mantel. And so, just as his wise father had done for him in days gone by, he set into motion the events necessary to achieve his royal intent. It was important to him that he leave his namesake more than just his wealth and title, for while these privileges had their place, they were no substitute for the greatest gift of all: A king's understanding. The wizened ruler knew that if he could successfully bestow this legacy upon his son that his kingdom would continue to be ruled righteously.

And so the king told his royal commissioners to consult the royal astrologers, who should survey the stars for the very best day to hold a special festival. Soon after, a royal decree went out across the land. All of the good and loyal citizens of his majesty's realm were royally requested, upon the fall of the next new moon, to present themselves and a gift of their choosing to the prince who would soon be their king.

Everything was now in motion. The stage was being carefully prepared. But even though the king had been through this play once before—with his father acting out the role he was now given to assume—he knew that there was no certainty to its final outcome. The heavens alone were the final author of this show of kings. He could only hope his son was ready to receive the lofty lessons being so carefully prepared for him.

As the big day drew near, the king began to spend more and more time spying on the castle's main courtyard. It was in the midst of being transformed into a fabulous multi-tiered outdoor theater. The special gift-giving ceremony was scheduled to be held there in less than three days, and he was watching in secret to see if the prince would start behaving as he expected and hoped he would. He was not disappointed by what he saw unfolding beneath him in the cobbled yard. During those few remaining days of preparations, his son was right down there in the thick of things, weaving in and out of the throngs, parading back and forth with a kind of self-abandonment that made him seem to almost float above all the activity taking place around him.

The king knew it must have appeared to everyone else

watching as though the young prince was just conducting one of his customary imaginary reviews of the Royal Guard. But the concealed monarch knew what was really occupying his young son's mind—and it had nothing to do with inspecting imaginary soldiers. No. The one and only thing dominating the mind's eye of the crown prince at the moment was the sweet image of a mountain of wondrous gifts that would soon be placed at his feet. He was counting his future riches and his father knew it with the same certainty as he knew there was a smile starting to spread across his own face. He was remembering how, once in his own not-too-distant past, he too had been the willing captive of the same strange sweet dream. And how, by the grace of his father the king, he was helped to awaken to something far better than this dream of dreams. Now he hoped to be able to do the same for his son.

Festival daybreak brought with it a fair sky and a warm sun. Before long the castle's outer courtyard was packed to capacity. After a few minutes of the required pomp and circumstance, the good king appeared to the spontaneous applause of his citizens. He greeted one and all and sincerely thanked them for coming. This, he told them, was a most auspicious day in the kingdom. And then, having said what he needed, he called for his son to be brought to him and to let the gift-giving procession begin.

Against a background of cheers, the bugles trumpeted and the prince was escorted out onto the center platform where he was seated in a special chair next to his father's throne. Then, one by one, in what seemed a line a mile long, the good people of the realm began making their presentations to the prince.

The first thing placed at his feet was a small bag of black beans. Then came some old Indian corn and a few misshapen gourds. The heir to the throne could not believe his eyes. He dared not voice it, but he thought surely some of the ministers of the court had staged an elaborate practical joke. But no one was laughing as one by one, the steady stream of people bearing gifts continued to pass before him. In front of him now was a wooden flute, several skinny hens, and a child's hunting bow fashioned from hand.

This had to be a mistake. He began to perspire and his face ached from holding a forced smile. Where were the chests of golden coins, the silken tapestries, the pouches of precious stones? Nothing that lay before him bore even the smallest resemblance to the treasures he had dreamt would be his on this day.

By the time just a few more minutes had gone by, the only thing that was keeping the prince in his seat—besides his father's evenly weighted hand firmly resting on his shoulder—was the occasional silver coin or two that were being dropped on top of the other gifts. But even their glint was quickly buried beneath a growing flood of potatoes, turnips and greens. How he hated turnips and greens!

As the parade of well-intended citizens continued to file by and leave their generous but common gifts, the king kept an ever-closer watch over the prince. He could see that his son was beginning to lose control of his carefully kept manners. No one else in the audience or on the stage understood the important nature of the events being played out before them. The king alone understood what was at the root of his son's deep disturbance and only he knew the one true solution.

But if the gift he intended to give his son was to make the maximum impression, his timing would have to be impeccable.

Finally the moment could hold no longer. He could feel the young prince about ready to bolt from his chair and run from the stage. Deliberately increasing the pressure of his one hand on his son's shoulder while raising the other to call for a temporary halt in the people's procession before them, he leaned over to the prince and began whispering. A hush fell over the entire court.

So clear were his father's words in his ear that for just a moment the prince thought to himself he had never heard this voice before. He couldn't help but listen.

"Son," his father spoke to him, "listen carefully to me. I want you to think for a moment about what I am going to tell you next, and then, if you still wish to leave the stage, I will not interfere."

The prince looked up and into his father's eyes and without saying a word he asked for the king's instructions. And though he heard what was said to him with his ears, it was his heart that listened.

"It is the common man who measures himself by the things that pass through his life—for it is only the common man who judges his own value according to what this life accidentally awards or denies. Your birthright is that of a king, but today you have acted quite common."

His father's words struck home like the sharp end of a lance—and they were all the more stinging because the prince knew them to be true. And then, suddenly, with no explanation, he felt strangely helpless. Of course his father had spoken the truth—and he did want to be noble—but on the other hand, piled right before his unbelieving eyes, were the bitter dregs of a dream that would never come again.

The prince wasn't sure in that moment what he was going to do. And just as he reached the point where he was certain there was no point in going on with his act—and that there was no one who could understand what he was going through—his father spoke to him once again. And when the king had finished, the prince realized that the only one who had failed to understand his position in life had been himself. And were it not for his father's words that day, he might have never seen it.

"My son, a true king is never concerned with what his subjects bring him, whether bags of silver or bags of straw, because *he knows he possesses the entire kingdom*. Look beyond this stage. Everything is yours. It always has been."

The prince slowly raised his head and looked out past the stage and over the crowds. At first he seemed to squint as though just coming out into the bright morning light. But, a moment later, his eyes were wide open and beaming. And then, as the king and all the court watched on, the prince raised himself from his chair and in a manner most befitting a king issued the decree: "Let the festival continue—on with the procession!"

The Secret Self is *your* royal nature. Like the kingly condition that it is, it knows about you what you have yet to learn about yourself. Let it reveal to you its secret kingdom. It belongs to you. You receive a portion of this kingdom each time you refuse to be captured by the common and choose instead in favor of the celestial. The stars are your birthright. We must look beyond the sparrow to the skies through which it wings.

Let life bring you what it brings. Receive each of its offerings with no concern for what you may think they say about you. Life is not trying to tell you anything about you. Life is trying to tell you about *it* and the vastness of its immeasurable riches that *already* belong to you. Yes. It is true. You already possess everything you will ever need, only it doesn't *feel* this way because you have been wrongly taught to cling to single things. Let go of these clinging thoughts and feelings that insist life be reduced to a hand-held jar. Just let them pass through you. Your willingness to allow life to pass through you brings with it the awareness that there is really no difference between you and it. This new understanding is the threshold to an eternal treasure chamber.

Now you are beginning to see, to realize, that you have always belonged to a ceaseless and ever-changing conscious Self. A Sacred Self whose very nature is *your* wealth. This is the Kingdom of the Secret Self. Let go and enter.

> *"There is no reason for this ecstasy—to have a cause for joy is no longer joy; it was simply there and thought could not capture it and make it into a remembrance—it came wave upon wave, a living thing which nothing could contain and with this joy there was benediction. It was so utterly beyond thought and demand."* —*J. Krishnamurti*

This Brand New Action Leads to the Wonderful Way

During a recent discussion group, Laura stated that she wished to spend the rest of her life discovering the truth about herself and the Secret Self. But, she went on to tell the class, she feared she had postponed her search for too long; that given her present set of circumstances, the outlook for breaking free of herself was bleak. At the root of her remarks was the following question: "How do I continue walking away from myself when my present world—and almost everything in it—is clamoring at me that it is pointless to even try and proceed?"

In the candor of Laura's comments, and the atmosphere they created, I noticed several other students nodding their heads in silent agreement. Without knowing it, they had almost all fallen into the waiting hands of one of the false self's most powerful deceptions: *Discouragement.* This hulking giant of self-doubt and despair lurks in the shadowy regions between what is True and what is *assumed to be.* And there is no way around it. But none is needed. Discouragement may seem like an inner Titan, but, in reality, it is only a big trick. Clearly, the time had come to shed some much needed light on this little-understood inner enemy of self-release. A candle is more powerful than a cannon in the dark.

Moments later everyone in the class, including Laura, was cheered and encouraged by the bright Truths revealed in the following remark—and we spent the rest of that evening's meeting in a vital question-and-answer session that carried all of us to a higher level of self-understanding.

We are disheartened and held captive by discouragement whenever we fail to remember that its only strength is in its ability to deceive. Its cunning is to convince us that it already knows the truth about why we can't take the next step beyond ourselves.

Question: Yes, what you say may be true for others, but what about the fact that I am locked into a difficult situation?

Until this condition changes, I am prevented from making the changes in my life that I know I must. What about that?

Answer: First, it is not the condition we find ourselves in that determines the work we can do to free ourselves. This is what the false self wants us to believe. Just the opposite is true. It is the work we do on ourselves that actually changes the conditions we are in, *whatever they may be*.

Question: What do you mean? How can working to let go of myself change the fact that certain conditions have a hold on me?

Answer: What you are calling a fact is only an assumption.

Question: How can you say that? You can't possibly know my circumstances.

Answer: We are all living under the same inner laws. We must never make the mistake of assuming that we know the whole truth about anything, since the truth is that there is always something beyond our present understanding.

Question: I agree with this, but how does knowing there is always something Higher change my circumstances?

Answer: From this Higher Understanding about the infinite nature of Truth you can take a completely new action towards your discouraging situation: You can dare to let go of what you are convinced is the truth about your sad state.

Question: That's a very different idea. I guess I am pretty sure about why I feel badly when I do. But what does letting go of this certainty accomplish for me?

Answer: Everything. By walking up to whatever may seem to be blocking your way—and daring to stand right there with a wish to go forward and the refusal to believe that you must go back—you have placed yourself right where Truth can begin working its wonderful way with you. From this point on, it is the Truth's responsibility to handle the rest of the difficulty.

Question: How does the Truth manage that? What

happens next?

Answer: If you will remain steadfast in your refusal to give up your wish for breaking through, the Truth will show you that what you had assumed was a solid wall of unyielding circumstance was really only a wall of discouraging thoughts created and constructed by the false self! Push against it once with the strength of your new understanding and it crumbles into the nothingness it always was. Before you awaits your next step up and out. Putting the Truth first in this way is the same as asking it to take you higher and higher. And it will.

Question: What exactly does it mean to put the Truth first? For instance, I always thought my right intention of waiting for a certain condition to improve—and then going to work on myself—was the proof that I treasured Truth above all else. But recent events and insights are trying to tell me this kind of thinking needs a closer look. Would you comment?

Answer: One day your sensing will be your certainty. To put the Truth *first* means just that. Thinking that we must wait for an improvement in our personal circumstances before we can let go and contact the Secret Self is not putting the truth first. This approach is putting our wish to *succeed* first.

Question: What is wrong with wanting to succeed? Isn't that the point?

Answer: Yes. But your inner success is Truth's responsibility, not yours. Your task is to understand this—and then to let Truth do for you what only it can do.

Question: Now that you point it out, there are a number of areas in my life dealing with relationships and other priorities where I suspect I've been less than truthful with myself. What do I do?

Answer: Just *start over* and then start over again. These two words, "start over," exemplify one of the most essential elements of the Truth, as well as stating to us its perennial instruction. There will be many, many times in our journey beyond ourselves where—for us to put the Truth first—it is going to mean seeing and admitting where we haven't been truthful with ourselves. Here is where we begin to understand some of Christ's higher intimations about the relationship between humiliation and salvation. "Blessed are the poor in spirit," begins to take on new meaning when we start to see just how "rich" our imagination has been concerning our truthfulness. Only after the Truth has taken the wind out of our self-made sails can we be carried safely home by the cosmic currents of the Secret Self.

Question: I find myself being sorry all the time—sorry for what I have done and sorry for myself, but nothing seems to change no matter how badly I feel. Is there no power for self-change in repentance?

Answer: Yes, there is. But when we do something wrong or hurtful to another, we are mostly sorry only for what we think our misplaced action may have cost us. Our sadness is over what we fear we have lost, including precious self-flattering self-images. The sorrow that leads to letting go and to true change of being is never over *what* we have lost, but *that* we are lost.

Question: Sometimes it feels like there is such a long way to go, and more and more I am not even sure which way that is. How can I be sure I am headed in the right direction?

Answer: There is no wasted effort if your aim is to walk away from yourself. Detecting a step in the wrong direction and then refusing to go that way is taking the next step in the right direction. Proceed positively in this way.

Question: Is there a summary of the Truth as it has been taught down through the ages?

Answer: The principle purpose of all True Teachings is to help us remember that we are not intended to remain as we are.

Question: I feel torn in two between what I want in my life and what I know in my heart I should be doing with it. What is going on? Can you help me see what I don't yet see?

Answer: We are born into this world with an invisible set of instructions folded into each of our tiny hands. One set of instructions compels us to prove to ourselves and to the world around us that we are strong, wise and worthy. The other instruction, the True instruction, beckons us to remember that we are here not to prove ourself but to discover it.

> *"But be ye doers of the word, and not hearers only, deceiving your own selves. For if any be a hearer of the word, and not a doer, he is like unto a man beholding his natural face in a glass; For he beholdeth himself, and goeth his way, and straightway forgetteth what manner of man he was. But whoso looketh into the perfect Law of Liberty and continueth therein, he being not a forgetful hearer, but a doer of the Work, this man shall be blessed in his deed."* James 22–25.

Follow These Fifty Secrets All the Way Home

I want to tell you something. Our travels together are just about over. But our journey beyond this self-limited life must continue. And that's why I have written this book about letting go. Letting go *is* the journey and it never ends. Never. It only begins—over and over again—each time we can glimpse something higher than our own painful certainty over who we think we are.

You can prove this to yourself. Take one of the inner lessons from any chapter section in this book that made a striking impression on you and go back and reread it once again. Make mental or written notes about the feelings it gives you. Notice everything you can about where within you this higher lesson seems to settle. Does it fill you with wonder? Does it cause an unfamiliar yearning or create a disturbance? Try and see as much as you can about it and yourself. Now, make this higher lesson the focus of your inner work for one week.

For instance, maybe you find the insight intriguing that we have unwanted and unrecognized inner guests who act invited but who are really inner invaders. Spend the following seven days with the intention of taking, as often as you can remember yourself, an inner inventory of exactly who is occupying your inner home. You may be surprised at the party being thrown at your expense.

Yes, it is disturbing. But your new awareness of this disturbance within you leads to a priceless realization that is beyond words: Now you know that it is *your* home and *not* theirs. You are on your way to true self-possession, because your work has revealed the *inner meaning* of this one higher lesson. You have moved at last from the intellect to the inspired.

When this miracle occurs, you will be breathless at the great depths of the lesson opening before you. And what scant seconds ago you were unable to see will now hold your complete attention. This moment of real inner-magic will happen with each and every lesson you return to until, one day, you realize with the same suddenness that it was never the lesson that was fathomless; it is your True Nature, the Secret Self that goes on forever. Now you are part of its invisible and powerful process.

The secrets we have uncovered in the last nine chapters have allowed us to gaze into the heart of some of the invisible worlds within ourselves. There we have discovered that the quality and even the content of our visible, physical lives, with all of their complicated relationships, is actually determined by the forces which rule these previously unseen inner realms. So it is here, within ourselves, that the work of letting go must be done. We know now that to fully see what is unwanted by us begins with revealing what is unknown *within* us. There is no other way. This is why we must persist within the inner work of our own individual inner journey.

The most amazing aspect about this special self-voyage is that each time we make it to yet another higher safe harbor within, we find that it isn't so much that we have been delivered to a place of increased personal power as we've been released from a long-held and deep-seated, mistaken belief in a powerless self! And as this false self is washed away in the light of our new understanding, along with it fades all of its equally false desires; desires that up to this point we had been convinced were our own necessary needs.

Because we persevered on the journey in, now we are well on our way out. Now we are happy to ask ourselves who *needs* to worry; to be anxious; to feel lonely or full of doubt; to express anger; to map the future or regret the past; to carry a grudge or plan some revenge? In fact, who needs to feel bad or sad over anything once it is understood that psychic suffering is just a symptom of spiritual short-sightedness? And that is truly all it is. Here now is the cure.

There is always something higher; a life beyond the limits of our present sight. But to see what is further we must be willing to lift our eyes from their present point of focus. This is letting go. Have no concern if at first you can't see. Vision *will* come. Here is an encouragement. See the truth of it and the truth of it will see you through your journey. Release always follows revelation and real revelation is always a glimpse of something that was only just out of sight.

Here are fifty ways to lift your inner eyes. I have placed them into four categories that in themselves tell The Secret of Letting Go.

See These Truths

1

You are always right where you need to be to take the next step beyond yourself.

2

Spiritual development is an equal opportunity for all.

3

Living in inner darkness, there are only two choices: The wrong one or the lucky one.

4

See the upset not as an exterior circumstance to be remedied, but rather as an interior condition to be understood.

5

All psychological conclusions are the fossilized assumptions of the false self.

6

Discouraging thoughts and feelings don't even know the truth about themselves, let alone what is around the corner.

7

Only an egotist likes to feel as if he is no one.

8

The very act of doing something for a reward is painful because it goes against your True Nature which is a reward unto itself.

9

Since spiritual awareness has no opposites, nothing can oppose it.

10

That bad feeling you don't want to feel is the feeling of not wanting that bad feeling.

11

That sentimental or sad remembrance is a memory, not a me.

12

Real love has nothing in common with any of its opposites—just as the sun is not dependent on the moon for its light or warmth.

Look Beyond Yourself

13.

Never hesitate to place yourself in a position where you don't know what to do.

14

If life knocks you flat on your back, open your eyes: Above you are the stars.

15

There is always something higher if you will only remember to keep your head held up.

16

When your destination is not of this earth, then nothing on this earth can disturb you.

17

Be the investigator, not the justifier.

18

To what you are connected is by what you are directed.

19

Truth has nothing to do with a self-pleased human being.

20

The Secret Self is a presence to perceive, not a prize to pursue.

21

A prayer for acceptance that isn't proceeded by a prayer for forgiveness is an act of arrogance.

22

You will know the Secret Self when you know that no man can help you, including yourself.

23

Never again help anyone to feel as though they have a right to feel badly.

24

Let the Truth awaken in you the remembrance that you are not here to remain you.

Just Let Go

25

Real change of self isn't found in some new way to think about yourself—but in the freedom from the need to think about yourself at all.

26

You can either die to experiences or from them.

27

Act from the self that is true and not from the self that is you.

28

Letting go is all about finding out who you are not, and having the courage to leave it at that.

29
Persistence is sticking with something until the stupidity gets out of the way.

30
The only way to produce more inner Light is by consciously sitting in the inner darkness.

31
To do the best you can do does not mean to suffer.

32
Jump into the Truth by being willing to jump out of yourself.

33
Letting go is not giving up; it is going up.

34
The Secret Self does not descend into an individual's life on any condition other than entire possession.

35
To be more alert, we need only listen for and then let go of the thoughts that steal our attention.

36
Set your course by no man and let no man set your course.

37
Let go of whatever it is.

Truth Always Triumphs

38
Whoever chooses Truth above *himself always chooses* for *himself.*

39

*Defeat is a memory —
it does not exist in real life.*

40

You can have the realization of helplessness without the feeling of helplessness.

41

When all has been done, patience is natural and has no strain.

42

To remain calm, we need only listen for and then let go of the anxious inner voices.

43

Living in the light of self-awareness there is only one choice, and it is always the right one, for consciousness never chooses against itself.

44

Whatever strength I add to myself becomes my greatest weakness, while whatever weakness I'll consciously endure will be replaced with a strength not my own.

45

When you know you are fully wrong, you will be standing at the gateway of real rightness.

46

*When life becomes your leader,
its spirit becomes your strength.*

47

*Truth pours in
as you pour out.*

48

You need neither the permission nor the cooperation of the world to put yourself last.

49

You can't silence yourself but you can allow stillness to show you its ways.

50

Never think that any situation is too difficult for Truth to Triumph.

Guy Finley lives and teaches in Merlin, Oregon. You are invited to write to him with your questions or comments about *The Secret of Letting Go.*

Guy Finley
Life of Learning Foundation
P.O. Box 170 LG
Merlin, Oregon 97532

A Special Message from Vernon Howard

When you begin to see that you have created your world in your own image, it will shock you. Here is a special exercise for you — for when you are pained. I can't tell you what a marvelous change this exercise will make in your life.

From this point on, every time you feel some hurt or inner agony, instead of thinking about the pain which you now do, you will do something else. Instead of directing your attention toward that sadness or disappointment, you are going to think about something else.

You are going to think, "I don't understand the pain."

Just think — "There is a darkness there, something that is lashing at me, and it hurts." But you are not going to get a false pleasure from the pain. You are going to go to the right department and say, "I don't understand the pain." THAT'S IT!

Then you never ever have to think another thought about the misery you are experiencing. You are through. You have done your part. THIS IS THE WAY OUT.

God Himself has just come to your rescue. This is what is authentically religious. God Himself says, "Don't think about and swim around in the suffering. Simply sit back in your chair, relax and say, 'I don't understand the anguish that is terrorizing my system.'"

If you don't understand it there is nothing YOU can do, is there? Then do nothing.

When we complain and cry and moan and groan and think, "How did I get into this mess," etc., nothing will change. With this exercise, you are putting yourself in an entirely different department and you will receive the products that that department has ready for you.

Do you want the product of not having to make worried decisions all day long? Just say, "I don't understand" — this crisis or that heartache that just came up. AND STOP. GO THROUGH YOUR WHOLE DAY *NOT* UNDERSTANDING IT.

It is our spurious understanding that gets us into the sorry inner mess in the first place. Don't be afraid to have no intelligence of your own. God is willing to make the grand magnificent substitute for you. God gives you His life in exchange for your life.

The majority of men and women sell their souls all day long in exchange for false, fleeting feelings of self-control. When you have true self-command, you never have to look for it or ever explain its absence to yourself.

If you are willing to say, "I don't understand anything at all about my life," your false understanding will fall away and in its place will be the insight from Heaven itself. That insight from a very High Place is all you need for this world and the next world. Go ahead and dare to let go.

A Special Note to the Reader

To receive your free inspiring poster, *10 Ways the Love of Truth Gives You a Fearless Life,* as well as free information about Guy Finley's books, tapes, and ongoing classes, send a self-addressed stamped envelope to:

Life of Learning Foundation
P.O. Box 10P
Merlin, Oregon 97532

Plus, you can receive a free copy of Guy Finley's powerful pocket guide book, *30 Keys to Change Your Destiny.* This amazing 28-page pocketbook of self-development exercises is filled with fascinating self-discoveries and help that work immediately. Send a self-addressed stamped envelope to the address above and please include $1 for shipping and handling. Outside the U.S., please send $3 U.S. funds.

Help spread the Light. If you know of someone who is interested in these Higher Ideas, please send his or her name and address to the Life of Learning Foundation. The latest list of Guy Finley's books, booklets, audio and video tapes will be sent to them. Thank you!